PASSAGE THROUGH TIME

A Milepost Guide
for the
Great Smoky Mountains Railroad

by
Michael George & Frank Strack

Layout and Cover Design
by Frank Strack
Cover photo taken near Ferguson Field by Robert Royem
Rear cover photo of
Conductor Jim Matthews by Frank Strack

Printed by
The College Press
P.O. Box 400 • 5047 Industrial Dr.
Collegedale, TN 37315

Acknowledgments

We would like to thank several individuals for their help with this book. They are not necessarily in order and we have probably left some out. Our apologies go to them.

Jack Dodd and Larry Petty at TVA have helped with maps and Fontana Dam information. Mary Ann Baily at the Federal Records Center helped with obtaining TVA photographs.

The retired railroaders that have helped are Ted Trexler, John Forster, Jack Hilton, Jack Hyatt, Robert Huffman, Emmet Earwood, and J. T. Earwood. J. T. is probably the only man alive that worked on the old Carolina and Tennessee Southern before Fontana lake was built, and he has provided insights that simply would not have been available from any other source. He has also generously provided photographs, timetables, and articles. Ed Griffin has supplied much information on locomotives.

Dale Roberts has supplied locomotive information and photographs. Ken Marsh has provided photographs and other valuable information. Bill Schaeffer at Norfolk Southern has provided old magazine articles on the Murphy Branch and other literature. Without Frank Ardrey, there would be very few photos from the late 40's and early 50's. The National Model Railroad Association's Kalmbach Memorial Library has helped with magazine articles and timetables.

Thank you to the Great Smoky Mountains Railroad staff who provided their time and supplied much information .

Other photo contributors include David Johnson, Jim King, Lavidge and Associates, Robert Royem, Carl Swafford, and Dale Taylor.

We would also like to thank Onecia George for providing Chapter 6. And most of all, thanks to God in Heaven for the talents and gifts He has provided.

Table of Contents

Introduction

The Southern Railway was once owner of a one hundred eleven mile stretch of railroad called the Murphy Branch. It extended from Asheville westward to Murphy. Originally called the Western North Carolina Railroad, the Southern gained control in 1894. Norfolk Southern now owns the line except for the western-most sixty-six miles. Of those sixty-six miles, Great Smoky Mountains Railroad owns and operates the line from Dillsboro to Andrews. The remainder of the line to Murphy is owned by the State of North Carolina.

This railroad extends across the mountains, deep valleys, and rivers of western North Carolina in some of the most beautiful scenery to be found anywhere. Geographically, the line begins on the west side of the French Broad River in Asheville and extends to Murphy, passing through Waynesville, Dillsboro, Bryson City, and Andrews. Originally, the goal was to reach Ducktown, Tennessee with its extensive copper deposits. When the Western North Carolina Railroad learned that the Marietta and North Georgia (Louisville & Nashville) was also heading to Ducktown, construction efforts were stepped up. Unfortunately, the M&NG won because the WNC never made it past Murphy.

Like arteries supplying the body with life-giving blood, The Murphy Branch was the artery that brought life to the many communities it served. For many years, it was the only access to these remote areas. Where previously this area was isolated and sparsely populated, it grew and prospered tremendously because of the railroad. At one time, the largest customer on the entire Southern Railway was located in Canton.

The Murphy Branch brought challenges to the men that operated it like no other part of the Southern Railway System. It was unlike any other part of the Southern and even the mighty Saluda (between Asheville and Spartanburg, SC) pales in comparison when one looks at the extreme operating conditions encountered on the Branch. Work on the Branch was so hard that some refuse to talk about it. Others loved their jobs with a passion. It may have been exhausting, but it was satisfying. Spending all day on the bouncing deck of a double-headed 2-8-0 steam engine shoveling by hand twelve to eighteen tons of coal on a hot summer day could break weak men; but railroaders could look forward to spending the night at the Henry House in Murphy, where there was always a full table of food awaiting them.

The grades encountered on this line were more like what would be found on a logging railroad than a common carrier. Balsam mountain grade, at 4.3 percent, was steeper according to the timetable than Red Marble grade at 4.2 percent. However, over the years the fills on Red Marble have settled causing the track to be steeper, possibly as much as 6 percent in places. Saluda grade is listed at 4.7 percent, but Southern Railway employee timetables listed tonnage ratings for a GP38-2 at 430 tons on Saluda and only 400 tons on Red Marble. In steam days, pushers were required at both Balsam and Red Marble, and westbound freights were triple-headed up the grade into the yard at Canton with sometimes a fourth locomotive pushing on the rear.

Only small locomotives could be used because of restricted bridges, close clearance tunnels, tight curvature, and light rail. Nothing larger than a 2-8-0 descended the west side of Balsam Mountain, and small drivered 4-6-2's were the biggest passenger power. They were reserved for branch line duty in mountainous areas and were splendidly painted in green and gold. There was hardly a spot in the entire line that was level. And, even though the builders took advantage of following rivers wherever possible, there were still grades in these "water level" areas. The rivers in these mountains aren't lazy and still, but are rushing torrents that attract whitewater enthusiasts from all over the world.

The area served by the Murphy Branch is rich in history. It is a story of determination and perseverance by strong men and women, good times and bad, tragedy and triumph, hardship and heroism. The stories are fascinating, the trials and troubles unbelievable. The entire Branch was built with convict labor, using hand tools and crude explosives. The few stretches of track that had ballast when the line was originally built used stone broken by sledgehammer. Many men lost their lives from sickness and accidents. When the work became miserably hard some convicts tried to escape, knowing they would be shot in the back.

This is not a book about a railroad with long freights and fast passenger trains. You certainly won't find any named passenger trains, nor will you hear about large, impressive stations with train sheds. The only train with a name was the Blue Goose, and it was a freight nicknamed by the firemen who were assigned to the second double-headed locomotive. They breathed smoke and steam and cinders and shoveled coal almost without stopping. The only automatic block signaling is in the first 1.3 miles, between Asheville and Murphy Junction.

This is, however, a book about a beautiful part of rural America. Where the trains seemed to have entirely too much motive power for the size of the train. Where the conditions were extreme and the demands great. Where the depot was the best place in town to be, especially when the train brought the mail. Where there were bridges and trestles and tunnels. Where twenty-four miles of track had to be relocated during the World War II Fontana Dam construction, and the government said do it without using one piece of new steel. Where the pace of life was a bit slower, and the people were friendly and helpful. The Murphy Branch was Class I railroading, but it had a distinct classic shortline personality.

Today, by riding Great Smoky Mountains Railroad, you have a chance to relive what it was like to travel on the Murphy Branch back in the 1940's with the comfort and safety of modern equipment. In the '40s, you would have had cinders blowing into your eyes from the open windows of non-airconditioned cars. If your train is pulled by steam locomotive number 1702, you won't have to worry about cinders - it burns oil instead of coal. Thus, if you are riding in an open car you can enjoy the scenic beauty and relax. In the '40s, dining cars were not used on the Murphy Branch. Now, you can enjoy a delicious meal in a luxurious dining car as you travel beside the Tuckasegee River.

You can follow your progress along the route by observing the mile-posts and finding the locations with the maps provided throughout the book. Something interesting about each mile of the railroad is listed in the text, mile by mile. Learn about the history of the equipment in which you are riding by looking at the roster information in the back of the book. You can also learn about the wildlife, flowers and trees along the railroad in the last chapter. But most of all, enjoy your trip. You will want to return many times to experience this great piece of American branchline railroading.

How To Use This Book

You will find this book very convenient to use during your trip on Great Smoky Mountains Railroad. The mileposts will be on the right side of the train as you head west from Dillsboro. They depict distances from Asheville. Thus, the mileposts numbers increase as the train heads west.

Each milepost on the railroad corresponds to one on a map and a block of text devoted to that milepost. Also, some photographs will feature the milepost symbol for even more information. The photographs may not always be in the same chapter as the map and text, but it should still be easy to locate the information on that milepost.

Some paragraphs may begin with a notation like 47.7. This means that the item discussed lies between Milepost 47 and 48, seven tenths of a mile from Milepost 47. There are no markers on the railroad to indicate these locations, but you should be able to get a feel after the first few miles of what one tenth of a mile is like. One tenth of a mile is 528 feet.

"Grade" refers to the steepness of the roadbed. A 4% grade means that the rails climb four feet vertically for every 100 feet of horizontal travel. Grades have an incredible effect on the pulling power of locomotives. For example, a 0.3% grade sounds very gentle: it is only a rise of 16 feet in one mile. However, the power needed to pull a train on a 0.3 grade is double what is required on level track. A 1% grade, then, more than triples the power required. Some of Great Smoky Mountains Railroad's track is well over 5%. With that in mind, it is obvious why the freight trains in the past had to have so many locomotives to move a very short train.

Curvature of the track is expressed in degrees. Normally one measures curves in radius, but when working in mountainous areas, it is not possible to establish a radius from the middle of a mountain. The curves are laid out using an instrument called a transit theodolite. The transit is set up on tangent (straight) track at the point where the curve begins, pointing towards the straight track. It is then rotated 180 degrees. If a ten-degree curve is required, the transit is rotated half that amount, or five degrees. Then, a chain exactly 100 feet long is stretched between the transit location and the point where the stretched chain meets the line from the transit. The transit is then moved to the new location and the process repeated. A ten-degree curve is considered fairly sharp, and would have a speed restriction of 30-35 miles per hour. Some curves on Great Smoky Mountains Railroad are very sharp, with one at 17 degrees. Great Smoky Mountains Railroad limits the speed to 20 mph on all trips.

The maps are laid out as if one is traveling from east to west, from Dillsboro to Andrews. On each map, as the train heads west, you will start at the right side and work your way to the left side. The railroad is indicated as a bold line. Contour lines are shown to give you a feel of the topography of the area. Where the lines are close together, the terrain will be very steep. More level areas are indicated by the lines spread far apart. An index to the symbols used on the map is included. The maps will overlap each other slightly to help orient you as you move from one map to another.

A milepost marker.

Switchstands and marker boards.

Whistle post indicating a grade crossing.

9

Provisional edition maps
New or replacement standard edition maps
Standard edition maps

Other land surveys:

Township or range line . . . .

Section line . . . .

Land grant or mining claim; monument . . . .

Fence line . . . .

ROADS AND RELATED FEATURES

Primary highway . . . .

Secondary highway . . . .

Light duty road . . . .

Unimproved road . . . .

Trail . . . .

Dual highway . . . .

Dual highway with median strip . . . .

Road under construction . . . .

Underpass; overpass . . . .

Bridge . . . .

Drawbridge . . . .

Tunnel . . . .

BUILDINGS AND RELATED FEATURES

Dwelling or place of employment: small; large . . .

School; church . . . .

Barn, warehouse, etc.: small; large . . . .

House omission tint . . . .

Racetrack . . . .

Airport . . . .

Landing strip . . . .

Well (other than water); windmill . . . .

Water tank: small; large . . . .

Other tank: small; large . . . .

Covered reservoir . . . .

Gaging station . . . .

Landmark object . . . .

Campground; picnic area . . . .

Cemetery: small; large . . . .   Cem   Cem   Cem

Provisional edition maps
New or replacement standard edition maps
Standard edition maps

RAILROADS AND RELATED FEATURES

Standard gauge single track; station . . . .

Standard gauge multiple track . . . .

Abandoned . . . .

Under construction . . . .

Narrow gauge single track . . . .

Narrow gauge multiple track . . . .

Railroad in street . . . .

Juxtaposition . . . .

Roundhouse and turntable . . . .

TRANSMISSION LINES AND PIPELINES

Power transmission line: pole; tower . . . .

Telephone or telegraph line . . . .   Tele

Aboveground oil or gas pipeline . . . .   Pipe
Above

Underground oil or gas pipeline . . . .   Pipel

CONTOURS

Topographic:

Intermediate . . . .

Index . . . .

Supplementary . . . .

Depression . . . .

Cut; fill . . . .

Bathymetric:

Intermediate . . . .

Index . . . .

Primary . . . .   No

Index Primary . . . .   Sho

Supplementary . . . .

MINES AND CAVES

Quarry or open pit mine . . . .

Gravel, sand, clay, or borrow pit . . . .

Mine tunnel or cave entrance . . . .

Prospect; mine shaft . . . .

Mine dump . . . .   Mine
dum

Tailings . . . .   Tailing

MAP SYMBOLS

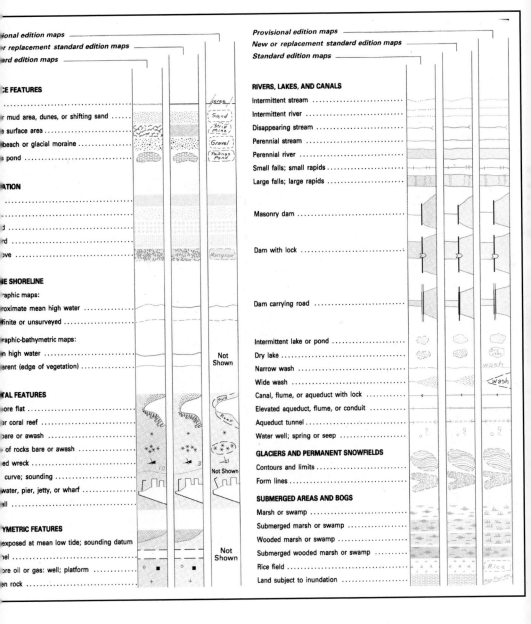

ional edition maps
r replacement standard edition maps
ard edition maps

Provisional edition maps
New or replacement standard edition maps
Standard edition maps

E FEATURES

r mud area, dunes, or shifting sand ......
e surface area ....
beach or glacial moraine ....
s pond ....

ATION

....
d ....
rd ....
ove ....

E SHORELINE

aphic maps:
roximate mean high water ....
finite or unsurveyed ....

raphic-bathymetric maps:
n high water ....
arent (edge of vegetation) ....

AL FEATURES

ore flat ....
or coral reef ....
bare or awash ....
of rocks bare or awash ....
ed wreck ....
curve; sounding ....
water, pier, jetty, or wharf ....
ll ....

YMETRIC FEATURES

exposed at mean low tide; sounding datum
nel ....
ore oil or gas; well; platform ....
an rock ....

RIVERS, LAKES, AND CANALS

Intermittent stream ....
Intermittent river ....
Disappearing stream ....
Perennial stream ....
Perennial river ....
Small falls; small rapids ....
Large falls; large rapids ....

Masonry dam ....

Dam with lock ....

Dam carrying road ....

Intermittent lake or pond ....
Dry lake ....
Narrow wash ....
Wide wash ....
Canal, flume, or aqueduct with lock ....
Elevated aqueduct, flume, or conduit ....
Aqueduct tunnel ....
Water well; spring or seep ....

GLACIERS AND PERMANENT SNOWFIELDS

Contours and limits ....
Form lines ....

SUBMERGED AREAS AND BOGS

Marsh or swamp ....
Submerged marsh or swamp ....
Wooded marsh or swamp ....
Submerged wooded marsh or swamp ....
Rice field ....
Land subject to inundation ....

This picture, taken on the Murphy Branch in the twenties, is at Dillsboro.
(Jim King collection)

Chapter 1

History of the Murphy Branch

Western North Carolina was an isolated area in the 1840's. The Great Smoky Mountains blocked passage to the north and west. Thousands of Blue Ridge peaks blocked passage to the south. To the east, the Appalachian Highlands made travel very difficult. In this region two hundred twenty-three peaks are over five thousand feet high. Forty-nine are over six thousand feet high, and Mount Mitchell, which is the highest peak east of the Mississippi, is nearby. Western North Carolina was an area rich in natural resources. There were abundant woodlands, with one hundred thirty species of trees; minerals, such as sand, gravel, copper, and olivene; and rich soil in the fertile valleys.[1]

There was a famine in 1845 that made the residents of Western North Carolina realize the degree of their isolation. Although Tennessee and coastal North Carolina did not suffer from the famine, it was impossible to ship crops into the area before they rotted. Only one road, Buncombe Turnpike, existed to connect Asheville with the outside world. It was not a safe route and many wagons were wrecked trying to bring in supplies. When the famine was over, the citizens had learned a hard lesson: it was no fun being hungry. The residents then put pressure on the North Carolina State Legislature to establish and subsidize a railroad.[2] The Western North Carolina Railroad was chartered by the State in 1855. Surveys began for a line that would connect Salisbury with Asheville. The charter read:

> "to construct a railroad, with one or more tracks, from the town of Salisbury on the North Carolina Railroad, passing by or as near as practicable to Statesville, in the County of Iredell, to some point on the French Broad River, beyond the Blue Ridge, and if the legislature shall hereafter determine, to such point as it shall designate, at a future session."

Four years later in 1859 it was amended to read:

> "from the point near Asheville to which the survey has already been made, extending west through the Valley of the Pigeon and Tuckasegee Rivers, to a point on the line of the Blue Ridge Railroad on the Tennessee River, or to the Tennessee Line at or near Ducktown, in the County of Cherokee."

During the six years before the Civil War, steady progress was made on the construction. But when the War started in 1861 there were still seventy incomplete miles to Asheville. In 1869, the line from Salisbury to Old Fort was finished. After that, several years passed with no construction and financial and legal problems. In February, 1877, construction west of Old Fort began using convict labor.[3] Major J.H. Wilson was put in charge. He finished the line to Asheville in 1879, in spite of tremendous civil engineering difficulties.[4] It took ten years of finding and blasting a usable right of way through the mountainous terrain. The original survey was useless, unsuitable even for a stagecoach line.

There was little gunpowder available. This made construction of the tunnels and cuts very time consuming. To remove rock, fires were built where the rock was to be removed. When the rock was hot, cold water was poured on it to crack the rock.[5]

The line was so curvy that eight complete circles could be made from the track between Milepost 113, a little west of Old Fort, to Milepost 122 near Swannanoa Tunnel if all of the curves were added together. Five tunnels were required. All of this was done with an average grade of two percent, gaining 891.5 feet of elevation.[6]

Unfortunately, little regard for life was shown to the convict laborers. The work was hard and the conditions poor. In 1872, five hundred convicts were released for track construction. They were divided into camps of one hundred and fifty men, each with captains, foremen, and guards. Each guard was responsible for ten or twelve men.[7]

The Western North Carolina hired an engineer named Cambar who came up with an explosive not using gunpowder. Nitroglycerine was mixed with sawdust and corn meal until a thick mash was created. This mixture was poured into drilled holes in rock and fuses were attached. Eventually, the mixture was refined to the point of putting it into oil-soaked paper cartridges. This resembled dynamite, and worked very well.[8]

14

Disaster struck on March 11, 1879. The Swannanoa tunnel was almost finished. Crews had been working from both ends and a locomotive had been brought up the mountain to begin track laying from Asheville to the tunnel. Engineer Jack Edwards was backing into the tunnel with empty flat cars to be loaded with rubble when the roof caved in. The engine was clear of the tunnel but rocks and earth covered the crew. Twenty-one men were crushed to death.[9]

More financial trouble plagued the line, and this time it was bought by William J. Best. He agreed to extend the line to Paint Rock, North Carolina to connect with the East Tennessee and Georgia by July 1, 1881. He also agreed to have rails to Ducktown, Tennessee by January 1, 1885.[10] Unfortunately, he couldn't live up to his agreement and it wasn't until January 28, 1882 that he reached Paint Rock. As soon as this was done, work began on what is now known as the Murphy Branch.[11]

Frank Clodfelter, an engineer, described the Murphy Branch's construction in this way: "The Murphy Branch is a dark (non-signaled) territory which we railroaders term the wagon-wheel line of the Carolina Division ...the railroad was hastily constructed along ancient Indian trails or cow paths."[12]

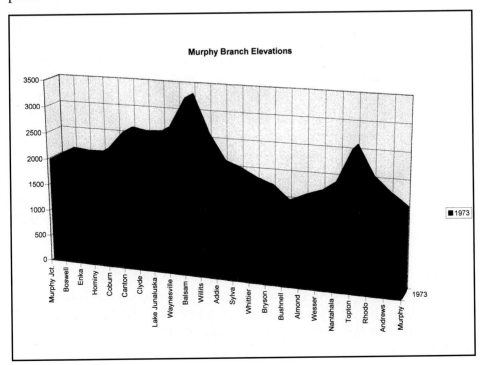

Best retained the use of convicts to build the line. The only stipulation was that he pay the State a total of $125.00 annually. Legislator Rufus Walker introduced a bill that provided pay for the convicts. This amount was $1.50 a day, which does not seem like much, but it added $250,000 annually to the budget of the Western North Carolina. This law meant more financial headaches for the struggling railroad. Mr. Walker owned a large plantation near Valley Town, a mile east of the present town of Andrews. The original survey had the line passing through the estate. Mr. Best was so upset by Mr. Walker's bill that he had the route resurveyed so that it bypassed the Walker estate.

This was really bad news for both men, because they both suffered from this action. Mr. Walker had no rail transportation for his plantation, but Mr. Best's decision cost him two more years of construction. The route change made steep grades necessary and a tunnel at Rhodo, three miles east of Andrews. To try to save construction time, he allowed the line to Murphy to have several steep grades that would greatly hinder operation.[12a]

In 1882, Best lost control of the Western North Carolina to the Richmond and Danville Railroad. Twenty-seven years had elapsed since construction started at Salisbury. Murphy was still one hundred miles away. The railroad was completed to Ford of Pigeon, which is now Canton, eighteen miles west of Asheville. Schedules were slow and most of the equipment dated to before the Civil War. Preliminary grading was completed halfway from Canton to Murphy at Wesser Creek. The crews were trying to follow the easiest route, using the Tuckasegee, Little Tennessee, and Nantahala rivers to take advantage of easier grades past Balsam Mountain, the first major obstacle past Canton.[13]

Balsam Mountain is where the tracks reached the highest elevation at 3351 feet. Southern Railway had a sign at this location stating that the Balsam Depot was the highest railroad station east of the Rockies. This statement was not true, however, as the Abingdon Branch of the Norfolk and Western had the honor of having the highest point on a standard gauge railroad east of the Rocky Mountains, at White Top, Virginia, elevation 3577 feet. Balsam Mountain required steep grades on both sides, but especially the west side, at four percent. In four miles, there is a seven hundred foot elevation change. A tunnel had been planned at the gap. This tunnel, just like another one further west, was not built because of unstable soil conditions.

The Valley River tunnel that has been renamed the Will Sandlin tunnel. The tunnel was required when builder William Best chose an alternate route because he became angry with an Andrews legislator that wanted the railroad to serve his plantation. (Michael George photo)

The Valley River bridge looking east toward the Will Sandlin Tunnel.
(Michael George photo)

About halfway between Canton and Balsam the town of Waynesville was established. It became a popular resort, just like several communities along the line. The railroad's presence made it easy for tourists from the lowlands to come enjoy the beautiful scenery and cool climate. Many famous inns and resorts were located throughout the area.

At the bottom of the western slope, a camp was set up. The wife of one

The Canton depot around 1915. The importance of the amount of industry in Canton is obvious by the large size of the depot. (Collection of Jim King)

of the crew superintendents was expecting a baby. Her name was Adeline. The site was named for her, although it was later changed to just "Addie."

Disaster struck again at a tunnel shortly after a young man by the name of Will Sandlin started working for the Western North Carolina. The Tuckasegee River makes a sharp bend just west of Dillsboro. To avoid this turn, the engineers built Cowee Tunnel. Every day, hundreds of convict laborers who were camped on the Dillsboro side of the river were ferried across the river to work on the tunnel. The ferry consisted of an old flat-bottomed boat. Since the current was strong, the railroad workers had set up a cable reaching from side to side. The men would work their way across holding onto the cable. On this particular morning, December 30, 1883, a Guard named Fleet Foster started across with his crew of nineteen convicts. He was in charge of some of the more dangerous criminals, so they were assembled into a chain gang. They had just started across the river when the rear of the boat began to take on water. The frightened men quickly moved to the bow, and the sudden shift of weight capsized the boat.

The convicts desperately struggled to keep their heads above water, but the heavy chains around their ankles prevented them from swimming. Unfortunately, they were all drowned except for Fleet Foster who was saved by a strong young black man, Anderson Drake. Mr. Drake might have been eligible for a pardon after this heroic deed, but Foster's wallet turned up missing after the incident. The wallet, containing thirty dollars, was found in Drake's clothing. Instead of being a free man, he was put back on the

18

Ks-1 No. 630 is coming across the high bridge east of Canton.

(Photo Collection of Jim King)

Canton switcher #599 is in front of the depot in 1947. The young fireman is Charles Cordell, who later became engineer and had a runaway train in Canton. The 599 spent over ten years as Canton switcher. *(G.P. Vance photo, Ken Marsh collection)*

GP30 No. 2572 in Waynesville on March 17, 1984.   *(Jim King photo)*

Southern Railway GP38-2 No. 5090 is westbound near Willits on May 2,1979.

(Jim King photo)

GP38-2 No. 5099 is at Addie on January 8, 1981.   *(Jim King photo)*

Something seems to have the crew's attention on train 17, at Willits. Quite possibly, it just has met the Blue Goose pictured on page 49 crossing the Tuckasegee River. May 23, 1947. (R.D. Sharpless photo, Frank Ardrey collection)

The depot at Addie, 1963. Note wooden semaphore through roof.

(Ken Marsh photo)

P-1 class #1297 on train 17, westbound to Murphy, in Canton on an April morning, 1939. (Norman Williams photo, collection of M.B. Connery, courtesy of Jim King)

chain gang and sent to the tunnel. Divers were brought in several days later to recover the nineteen drowned convicts.[14] The bodies of the men were buried on a hillside above the tunnel in an unmarked grave. The tunnel has continued to be a problem over the years, with steam engines and diesels hitting rock slides inside. The late 1960's saw a sixteen-car freight avoid disaster when it stopped barely in time to avoid a cave-in.[15] Traveling east on the railroad, an engineer had to negotiate a steady climb from Bryson City to Balsam, and trains were prone to stall in the tunnel.

Stalling in the tunnel could be quite dangerous, because the steam and hot smoke made breathing nearly impossible. Life was especially hard on the crew in the second steam engine, since they received twice the dose of steam and smoke. In later years, the second locomotive was placed in front of the caboose in Bryson City for trips through the tunnel. This made it a little easier on the crews. At Addie, the locomotive was placed back on the front of the train.

The Murphy Branch may be best known for its Red Marble grade between Nantahala and Topton. This steep grade, at 4.2%, was required to climb out of the Nantahala River gorge. By the time the work started on

23

Locomotive #630, Ks-1, is in Asheville in November 1938. Ks-2 #573 is behind it. Notice how the cylinder covers are painted. During this period, locomotives were assigned to specific engineers. Each locomotive had unique features.

(Norman Williams photo, Ken Marsh collection)

this grade, Will Sandlin had been promoted to grade foreman. The construction crews were almost to the top of the grade when Richmond and Danville officials doubted the original survey. They brought an "expert" civil engineer named Hankins to reevaluate the route up the mountain. After his examination, a new survey was ordered by the officials.[16]

Hankins immediately ordered the crews to start over at Nantahala, but his hasty instructions were given without taking the time to do soil content analysis. His new survey had the line located about fifty feet below the previous excavation and called for a tunnel at the top to reduce the grade. Will Sandlin knew grading the new route would be dangerous, because they would be undercutting the previous fills on the mountain side. However, work was ordered to progress at a rapid pace.[17]

The tunnel was planned for the summit at Red Marble Gap. It would have been at least five hundred feet long. Will Sandlin's father was in charge of blasting. One day, Hankins sank a test shaft in the middle of the bore. The result brought bad news to the Richmond and Danville officials. The test showed a pool of white mud under Red Marble Gap. This white mud had been encountered before, in Mud Cut between Old Fort and Ridgecrest.

Opposite Page: The location is Balsam, the date is unknown. Train is headed east led by consolidation 857.   *(Hugh Comer photograph, collection of Jim King)*

The Balsam depot claimed to be the highest one on a Class 1 railroad in the Eastern United States, unfortunately this was an incorrect statement. The Balsam Mountain Inn, still in use today, is in the background. The depot still exists, but has been moved. Photo taken in 1959-61. *(Jim King collection)*

The jellylike mud would boil up under the tracks, raising the level many feet. The roadbed was always spongy here. The first surveyor, Jim Coleman, had staked his original line at the steep 4.2% to avoid the mud. He had seen evidence of the white mud and was trying to avoid it. Coleman had experienced firsthand the problems with Mud Cut. If Hankins had consulted with the mountain engineer, much work and money could have been saved.[18]

The construction crews returned to Nantahala a third time and returned their efforts to the original line. They were already two years behind schedule and Murphy was still twenty-eight miles away. The winter of 1885-86 was an especially hard one. At one time, three feet of snow covered the ground. Mr. Sandlin was camped toward the top of the mountain with one hundred fifty men. In the gorge below, several other companies were camped. When the spring thaw started, the creeks and rivers were filled to overflowing. The currents destroyed fills and trackage. Suddenly, Mr. Sandlin found himself stranded on the mountain with no source of supplies. Bryson City, then known as Charleston, was the closest town, but with the condition of the tracks and trails in the area, the trip would take several weeks. To get to Murphy was even worse, since there were no established roads.[19]

The crew of convicts, guards, and foremen survived by hunting small game. But wild game alone did not provide a balanced diet, and men were getting sick. Time spent on the job was cut to four hours a day. Steve Whittaker, who lived on a farm near Andrews, brought twenty bushels of corn and other supplies to the camp. He used a wagon pulled by four oxen. This helped, but before he arrived nineteen men died from scurvy. They were buried close to the camp, a little west of Hawknest Trestle. This trestle, near the Graham County interchange, was filled in during the late 1940's.[20]

Hawknest Trestle was Will Sandlin's first major project. It was four hundred feet long and forty-three feet high, built in 1887. Will was only twenty years old when he was assigned the project by Hankins. He had never seen a set of blueprints. This trestle and a deep cut at Topton were the only remaining obstacles to the completion of the Red Marble grade. Sandlin spent hours studying the plans. When he was comfortable, he took work crews and an oxen team down the mountain. He selected trees that the workers felled and sawed into timbers right where they fell. Then the oxen would take them to the building site. The young engineer was uneasy when the first bent was raised, but his careful work paid off. The trestle ended in perfect alignment.[21]

Graham County Shay #1925 and caboose #10, an ex-L&N caboose that probably came to the Graham County by way of Blue Ridge and Murphy, at Bear Creek in 1980.

(Jim King photo)

The cut at Topton was finished about the same time as the trestle. It was forty-three feet deep, but the white mud was to prove itself a further hindrance. The cut was so deep that the workers had cut right into the mud. Crosstie after crosstie was thrown in the mud to try to give some stability to the mass. Finally, the engineers were satisfied that the roadbed was stable. The depth of the cut has continued to shrink over the years due to the continued filling with mud. [23]

The Western North Carolina finally reached Murphy in 1891, six years late. Murphy was to be as far as the tracks would go, however. The Marietta and North Georgia had pushed narrow gauge rails into Ducktown in 1885. The rails would eventually go all the way to Knoxville. A branch was built from Blue Ridge, Georgia to Murphy. There were plans to go even further into North Carolina, possibly to Asheville. But a financial panic in 1892 helped the Marietta and North Georgia decide Murphy would be just fine as the eastern terminal. Asheville was to remain a one-railroad town. Rather than the Western North Carolina tapping into the rich copper mining areas around Ducktown, it was the Marietta and North Georgia. There was interchange traffic between the two railroads in Murphy. This was easier after the Marietta and North Georgia widened its rails to standard gauge.

A large celebration in the form of a barbecue welcomed the arrival of the first Western North Carolina train in Murphy in June 1891. It did not turn out to be a happy event for the weary railroaders, though. Tables had been set up to seat about one hundred fifty men. The convicts patiently waited in orderly groups. When the announcement was made for the guests to be seated, there was a stampede of local residents trying to push their way to the tables. A fight erupted and the railroaders were driven off without eating a bite. Will Sandlin was deeply disappointed in the behavior of the locals. He knew his men were anxiously awaiting the dinner and had done no wrong.[24]

Arrival of the railroad into Murphy did not mean the work was finished. The rails into Murphy had been hastily laid, no ballast had been used, and the roadbed was rough. Derailments were common. Sandlin was put in charge of putting in stone culverts and abutments.

Only three years after completing the Murphy Branch, the Richmond and Danville lost control. This time the new owner was the Southern Railway.

Other shortlines that connected with the Murphy Branch were the Ritter Lumber Company, the Alarka Valley, the Carolina and Tennessee Southern, Smoky Mountain, Sunburst, B&B, Tuckasegee Southeastern, and Appalachian. Some narrow-gauge lines reached elevations of over five thousand feet in the high country.[27]

The Murphy Branch was prosperous, hauling the timber products, agricultural items, and the general supplies necessary to sustain the tiny communities along the line. However, only being a branch line, it was not maintained nearly as well as the other divisions, and with the steep grades, sharp curves, and light rail, it had only the smallest locomotives. The smallest locomotives were generally the oldest and most worn. By 1907, the line had really fallen into disrepair. Derailments were common, and to quote George Sandlin: "for a while our trains were on the ground just as often as they were on the crooked, worn-out rails. But we worked on. We got more cussings than a pirate crew as we swore and sweated blood to put cars back on the right-of-way."[28]

On January 1, 1907, the Branch was reorganized into the Murphy Division. Headquarters were moved to Bryson City. For the next eight decades,

Engine #1256 sits in the afternoon sun in front of the Murphy depot. It has been turned on the wye and is positioned for its trip east in the morning. Note the two rerail frogs on the tender frame. The date is May 23, 1947.

(R.D. Sharpless photo, Frank Ardrey collection)

the line continued to serve the communities along its route. However, changes began to occur that made some question the future of the Branch.

A closer look at the operations in Murphy sheds some light on how things began to deteriorate. There is only a one hundred fifty-foot elevation change in the fifteen miles between Andrews and Murphy, making this the easiest portion of the Branch to operate trains on. The grade is gently rolling and roughly parallels the Valley River. Three miles east of Murphy, there is a 174-foot-long timber trestle forty feet high that crosses Marble Creek. As the tracks come into Murphy, the line crosses the Valley River on a through truss bridge. It is apparent after viewing this bridge why small Pacifics were the heaviest power allowed on this end of the line. Below this bridge the Valley River flows into the Hiwassee River. The Southern lost a great deal of real estate in Murphy when Hiwassee Dam was built. There

The depot at Murphy, Oct. 1967, looking east.   *(Ken Marsh photo)*

were several tracks on the north side of the Valley River. The depot was located across the river in town. The L&N also had a depot in Murphy that still stands. There was a small yard used for interchange traffic between the two railroads. In the mid-forties, twelve to fifteen cars were picked up by the Southern every day. There was a wye large enough to turn the entire passenger train. This saved a significant amount of switching for the train crew.

By the early 1980's, interchange traffic with the L&N had dropped drastically. Without the interchange traffic, the L&N didn't have much reason to come to Murphy. Only one train a week was run from Blue Ridge to Murphy on Mondays. Pulpwood was the only freight shipped between Murphy and Mineral Bluff. L&N's new owner, the Seaboard System, had little patience for unprofitable branch lines so the rails were soon pulled. The deck plate girder bridges across the Hiwassee River were removed also. These were somewhat unique since the points of a turnout extended onto the bridge on the east end. Ironically, the L&N depot still stands, but the Southern one is long gone.

Switching the freight train in Murphy could take several hours. Usually, one of the double-headed steam engines was uncoupled and set off. The other locomotive would do the switching. The crews would alternate which locomotive was cut off to keep the workload evenly distributed. The freight

The truss bridge over the Valley River in Murphy. The depot is around a turn, past the overpass in the background. Note the light duty construction. (Jim King photo)

didn't run on Sunday so whoever was assigned the job on Saturday had to lay over an extra day.

In the forties, the twelve hour law limiting the amount of time a railroader could work was not in effect. Then, crews could work sixteen hours. Sixteen hours made for a very long, hard day. It would be late at night sometimes before the crew finished switching. The railroad did not provide a place to spend the night, so most men went to the Henry House or an old hotel on a back street.

The Henry House was up the hill in town on a main street. Adeline was a black woman who cooked meals for the railroaders. Four or five older women helped her. No matter what time the crews arrived, there was always hot food on the long tables. Large stoves were in the kitchen, and the ladies fried apples, cooked sausage and biscuits, and made gravy and other fine food. Upstairs were rooms for sleeping. A man named Henry bootlegged white liquor once in a while. The railroaders would ask "Henry, is the old hen settin' today?" If he said no, that meant there was no moonshine. If he said "yeah, she's a cluckin" that meant he had a supply.

Murphy, for a small town, was full of steam engines at night. The passenger train locomotive was there, the two 2-8-0's from the freight were there, and in the forties, the L&N mixed train laid over also. The Southern had a caretaker to watch the locomotives. He kept coal in the fireboxes and water in the boiler all night. He also had to cut coal so the fireman could access it easily in the morning. Towards the end of steam operations, a small coal loader was put in Murphy so the tenders could be filled.

31

No. 1318, L&N H-29 2-8-0, is on the interchange track with the Southern in Murphy in 1938. The L&N depot is on the right and the Southern's yard is to the left behind the tender.
(Norman Williams photo, collection of Ken Marsh)

There were several industries in Murphy. Pulpwood was loaded, there was a pallet manufacturer, a propane dealer, and a couple of oil companies. Boxcars carried feed to be unloaded at the team track. Crossties were made at a lumber mill. Sand was unloaded at a special ramp.

In 1937, the freight train left town first at 6:00 a.m. The passenger train left at 8:00 a.m. The passenger train arrived at 1:45 p.m. By 1944 there was only one passenger train running on the Branch. It left Murphy at 7:15 in the morning with the train from Asheville arriving at 2:15 p.m. Construction of better highways in the mountains made the automobile more and more practical in western North Carolina. Great Smoky Mountains National Park, dedicated in 1940, was conveniently accessed by car. The Blue Ridge Parkway was under construction also. People enjoyed the independence the automobile provided.[29] As a result, regularly scheduled passenger operations stopped on July 16, 1948.[30]

The L&N Murphy depot on March 9, 1986. The turnout extends onto the plate girder bridge over the Hiwassee River. The track to the left leads to the Southern yard. (Jim King photo)

L&N GP-38 4000 is in the Southern yard at Murphy, March 10, 1979.   (Jim King photo)

Rio Grande Caboose on siding at Bryson City, July 2000.   **(Frank Strack photo)**

Depletion of timber resources in the area and the completion of Fontana Dam caused traffic to begin slowing down on the Murphy Branch in the late forties. By 1985, traffic had dropped significantly. In 1980, 2,239 carloads moved over the Branch. In 1987, only 817 carloads had been moved. The last three years of operation by the Norfolk Southern saw two and three unit locomotives operate from Waynesville to Andrews. Only occasionally did trains go into Murphy. Traffic on the west end of the Murphy branch was usually a maximum of five cars per train. The operation of three loco- motives on a five car train is not cost effective.

Maintenance costs were high on the Branch. The extreme curvature of the track is expensive to maintain. There are thirty-four bridges with a combined length of 4800 feet between Dillsboro and Murphy. Speed limits had been twenty-five miles per hour for several years, and from Andrews to Murphy the speed limit was ten miles per hour. The 80 and 85 pound rail was manufactured between 1903 and 1926. There was some 75 pound rail that dated back to 1894.

The final blow to the west end of the Murphy Branch was when the Champion paper mill in Canton converted from pulpwood to woodchips in 1984. The tunnels at Dillsboro and Rhodo would not allow high cube woodchip cars without extensive work to either lower the roadbed or raise the ceiling. Pulpwood had been the major source of carloadings on the west end, and now it would have to be trucked to Canton. Norfolk Southern filed for abandonment of the western sixty-seven miles between Dillsboro and Murphy in 1988.[31]

Several operators had plans to continue freight service and operate passenger excursions. However, none had an acceptable financial plan. At the last minute the State of North Carolina decided to purchase the railroad. The North Carolina Department of Transportation purchased the line on July 19, 1988 for $650,000. After more than one hundred years, the state again owned the Railroad. A new company was formed called Great Smoky Mountains Railway Inc. Great Smoky Mountains Railway leased the line at $40,000 per year plus a percentage of gross revenues for twenty-five years.[32]

The purchase and lease agreements stipulated that freight service would continue and passenger trains in the form of excursions would be run.

Great Smoky Mountains Railway started operations with two GP-9 locomotives. One was from the Union Pacific Railroad and one came from the Burlington Northern Railroad. Passenger equipment consisted of a few coaches and freight cars which were converted to open passenger cars. The railroad began accumulating cabooses from many different railroads. These cabooses also served to haul passengers.

By 1995 the Great Smoky Mountains Railway was operating four diesel locomotives and one steam engine. The steam engine is an ex-Army Baldwin locomotive that served during World War II. Built in 1942, it was converted to burn fuel oil so passengers don't have to contend with cinders. Two GP-7's, numbers 711 and 777, came from the Chicago and North Western. The railroad also owns two GP-35's from the Norfolk and Western. Number 711 has been upgraded to a GP-9. The crews prefer the GP-7's on the grades because they are less likely to slip. One GP-7 can handle three one hundred ton grain cars up the Red Marble grade. The diesels have been renumbered to match steam locomotives used in the past on the Branch.

Great Smoky Mountains Railway leased two CF-7 locomotives from the Lone Star Railroad in Texas in the early 1990's. CF-7s were converted from old Sante Fe F-7s. F-7s were streamlined diesel locomotives. The paint scheme shown was used for the first twelve years of Great Smoky Mountains Railway operations. (David P. Johnson photo)

Passenger equipment consists of restored coaches, crown coaches, club cars, dining cars, open cars, and the cabooses. The club and dining cars came from the Seaboard and Atlantic Coast Line railroads.

Great Smoky Mountains Railroad offers several excursions. One is from Dillsboro to Bryson City and return. One trip to the Nantahala Gorge departs Bryson City on the relocated line and has a layover at Wesser for an hour, then returns to Bryson City. Some excursions follow the entire line from Dillsboro to Andrews with a return trip by bus. Another excursion leaves Dillsboro and goes to the Nantahala River Gorge, mp 86.5, and returns to Dillsboro.

Great Smoky Mountains Railroad also offers several unique excursions. The Raft'n' Rail departs Bryson City and arrives at the Nantahala Gorge. An eight mile raft trip down the Nantahala River follows. A picnic lunch is included and the return trip to Bryson City is by bus. A two and a half

How much better can life get? Riding in a caboose, with a thumb to suck on, a soft blanket, and Mom's lap. *(Michael George photo)*

hour Gourmet Dinner Train departs Dillsboro on Saturday evening. Special Mystery Theater Dinner Train excursions, performed by local professional actors, are offered throughout the year. There are also special trains at Halloween, Christmas, and New Years Eve. The Railroad offers photo specials as fund-raisers to various National Railroad Historical Society Chapters.

Great Smoky Mountains Railroad track begins in Dillsboro at milepost 47. They have trackage rights over the Norfolk Southern to milepost 45 in Sylva. This is where the two railroads interchange traffic. Norfolk Southern still services the industries between Sylva and Dillsboro including the Jackson Paper Manufacturing Company.

Safety is the primary concern in operating trains over the Great Smoky Mountains Railroad. Someone is at the steps on every train to assist passengers. Before any train departs, a Hi-Rail truck leaves and makes an inspection of the track, looking for rocks, trees, or any other problem. All locomotives carry chain saws and chains for removing anything that might fall on the track after the inspection truck passes. The speed limit on pas-

Conductor Jim Matthews at Bryson City, July 2000.
(Frank Strack photo)

senger trains is twenty miles an hour, but they are usually operated at fifteen or sixteen miles an hour. In sharp curves and other high-wear areas, the 80 and 85 pound rail has been replaced with heavier rail.

The locomotives, cars, and track are maintained to high standards. Nine trackside lubricators have been added in sharp turns. Norfolk Southern had only three. Another rail lubricator is installed in the back of a Hi-Rail truck and the entire line is lubricated at the start of each season once a week for three weeks. After that, the lubrication schedule changes to once a month. This greatly reduces the amount of wear on the rail. It also reduces the wear on locomotive and car wheels. A program has been started that replaces light rail in high-wear curves with heavier rail. Large stones from the quarry at Talc Mountain have been added in the Nantahala Gorge where the embankments were prone to wash out. Once a year, the tender is removed from the steam engine and coupled to a diesel. The tender is filled with water. A high pressure pump and hose are attached and all culverts on the railroad are washed free of debris. This has stopped flooding and resulting track damage. Norfolk Southern had deferred maintenance on bridges and culverts before they filed for abandonment. Several culverts were totally blocked. The bridge over the Tuckasegee at Dillsboro has been totally redecked and one concrete pier has been reworked to make it significantly stronger. Many ties have been replaced on the Little Tennessee

River crossing of Fontana Lake. Several trestles have been rebuilt with heavier timbers.

In 1996 Great Smoky Mountains Railway purchased the line between Dillsboro and Andrews from the State of North Carolina. The State owns the track between Andrews and Murphy, which does not see any use.

The Great Smoky Mountains Railway was purchased by American Heritage Railways of Florida. Ownership took place December 23, 1999. American Heritage Railways owns the Durango and Silverton Narrow Gauge Railroad in Colorado. The name was changed to Great Smoky Mountains Railroad. The color scheme of the equipment was changed from the previous red, yellow, and blue to a more traditional Tuscan Red and Rio Grande Gold. Many other improvements have been made to track and facilities.

The future looks bright for the Great Smoky Mountains Railroad. Completion of a four lane highway from Atlanta to Highway 19\74 between Andrews and Murphy is planned. This should bring more tourists into these areas. The Bryson City and Dillsboro based departures currently have the greatest patronage.

Great Smoky Mountains Railroad rebuilt this 130 ft. long wood trestle at milepost 98.6 in July 2000.   *(Michael George photo)*

When passenger operations ceased on the Murphy Branch in 1948, it was the end of an era. The trains had made it possible for the people in these tiny communities to have access to the rest of the world. They probably did not realize how unique the railroad was that served them. They took for granted the service provided by the Southern Railway, and it possibly never occurred to them just how beautiful and scenic their homeland was. Now, nearly fifty years later, the opportunity exists to ride on this mountain railroad and experience the beauty of the country, the incredible operational demands placed on the railroad and its operators, and the peacefulness of the rivers.

P-1 class 1288 is at the Andrew's depot circa 1946. Notice the truck loading mail, the engineer oiling the locomotive, and the express boxcar behind the truck.

(photo courtesy of Dale Roberts)

Chapter 2

The Milepost Guide

47 Beginning of Great Smoky Mountains Railroad's track

Great Smoky Mountains Railroad's track begins at Milepost **47**. This milepost is east of Dillsboro. You will not see this point since the train originates at the Dillsboro depot, or mile **47.7**. Freight traffic that comes from the Norfolk Southern is left in Sylva, at Milepost 45. Great Smoky Mountains Railroad has trackage rights from Milepost 47 to 45 so the freight traffic may be picked up. Freight cars from Great Smoky Mountains Railroad are left for Norfolk Southern to take east to Asheville.

There is a famous landmark in Dillsboro called the Jarrett House. It was built by William Allen Dills in 1884, two years after the Western North Carolina Railroad came to this town. Obviously, Dillsboro is named after

Jarrett House, Dillsboro, NC, September 2000.   *(Frank Strack photo)*

Mr. Dills. The hotel was originally called the Mount Beula Hotel. It soon became the popular place for both train crews and passengers to eat. When the passenger train stopped on its way to Murphy, a twenty-minute break was given for passengers to eat. It became so popular that passengers began having the agent at Balsam telegraph their dinner reservations to Dillsboro! The Hotel gained popularity when two ladies from Edenton spent several

(49) *Left: Steam engine 1702 crossing the Tuckasegee River on the Cowee Trestle.*
Bottom: Diesel No. 777 coming through the Cowee Tunnel in Sept. 2000.
(Frank Strack photos)

weeks there in the summer of 1886. It seems that these ladies were the first women to be seen in this area smoking cigarettes. Soon, the whole town was talking about it. In 1894 the Hotel was sold to Frank Jarrett, who changed the name to The Jarrett Springs Hotel. There was a sulphur spring at the rear of the hotel. Supposedly, sipping the spring water would give the body "new vigor." The restaurant was famous for the meals cooked by the innkeeper's wife, "Miss Sallie." Mr. Jarrett became widely known for his unique method of curing hams. He operated the hotel until he died. In 1950 W.B. Faw purchased the property. He gave the hotel its current name, The Jarrett House. In six years he sold it to Mr. and Mrs. Silvis and Florence Harris. In 1960 it was bought by the Lowes. It now belongs to Jim Hartbarger, his wife Jean, and their two sons. They are committed to continuing the fine meals that have built such a fine reputation for the Jarrett House. It was designated a National Historic Place in 1984.

This whistle stop shed was probably moved to Dillsboro after the depot was destroyed. June 16, 1976. Notice the gasoline prices.   *(Jim King photo)*

47.7 Dillsboro Depot
The train will depart to the west from here. The track descends at approximately 0.5%. The elevation is about 1900 feet.

48 Great Smoky Mountains Railroad Shops and Yard
Right after passing the Highway 441 underpass, Milepost **48** is on the

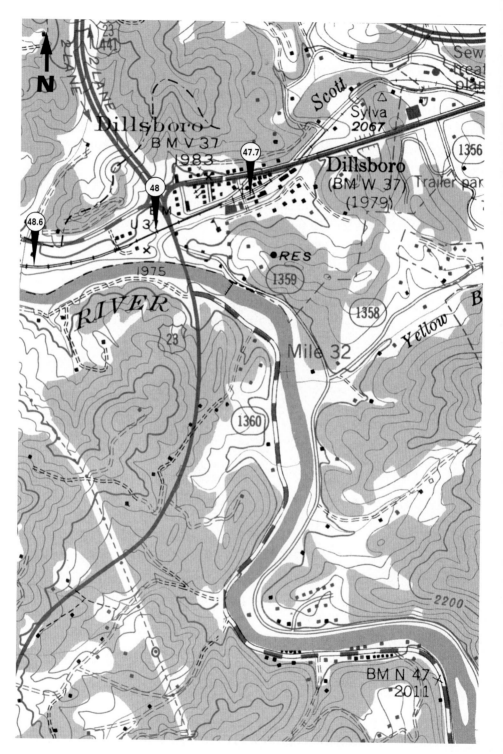

(47) *Southern GP30 No. 2560 is eastbound at milepost 47 in 1981. This now marks the beginning of Great Smoky Mountains Railroad's track.* *(Jim King photo)*

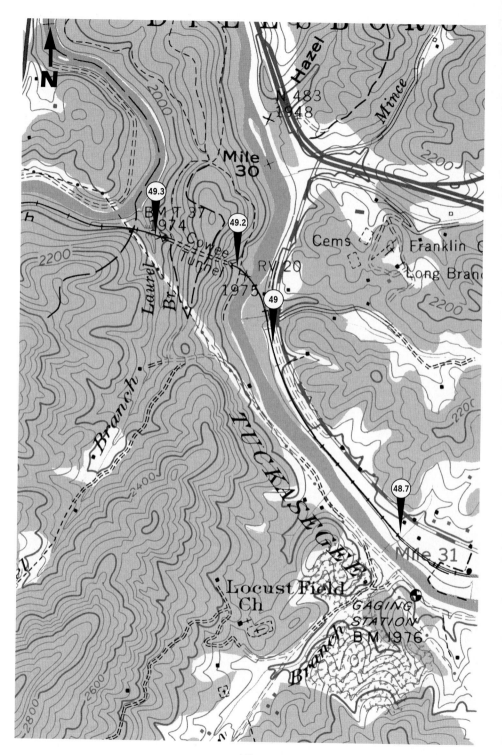

right. The Great Smoky Mountains Railroad shops begin here. The siding to the left has been installed by Great Smoky Mountains Railroad. It is called the "Sarge" track, named after James Revis, a retired Southern Railway track maintenance man who also worked for Great Smoky Mountains Railroad. The shop building on the right is an old olivine mine. Olivine is a magnesium iron silicate, transparent green in appearance, and used as a gem. All maintenance and repairs to Great Smoky Mountains Railroad equipment is carried out at this location.

48.8 "Fugitive" Filming Location

The bus and train wreck in the film *The Fugitive*, starring Harrison Ford and Tommy-Lee Jones, was staged at this point. This was the most dramatic train wreck scene ever filmed in motion picture history. On your left, you can see two diesel locomotives, one bus, and remnants of another bus. A special track was built to the left of the mainline to stage the train wreck. The bus was rolled down a bank on the right side. The track begins a 0.7% climb to the deep rock cut at mile 49. The left hand curve through the cut is 12 degrees.

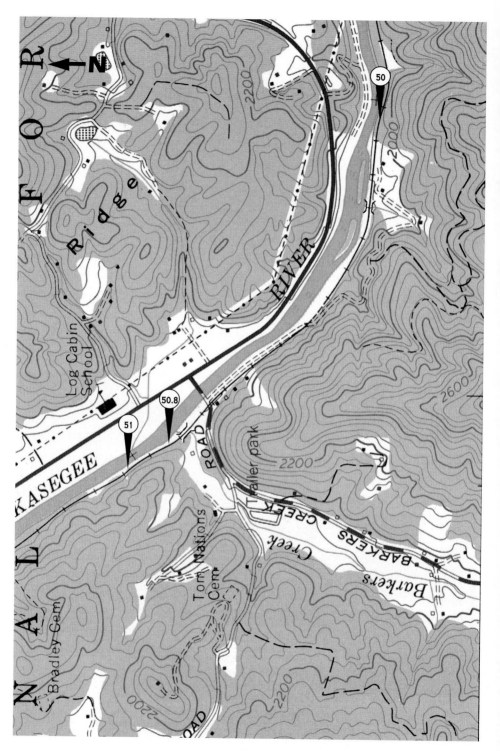

49 *Ks-2 #573 is coupled behind Ks-1 #712 on May 23, 1947. They are eastbound, crossing the Tuckasegee River west of Dillsboro. They have just come through Cowee Tunnel.*
(R.D. Sharpless photo, Frank Ardrey collection)

49 Tuckasegee River Crossing and Cowee Tunnel

Right after exiting the cut, you will cross the Tuckasegee River for the first time. The crossing is made on three steel deck plate girder bridges 197 feet long. Immediately after crossing the river, the train enters the Cowee tunnel. See Chapter 1 for historical information about the building of the tunnel. You will enter the tunnel in an 8 degree left turn. In the last one third of the tunnel, the curve swings to the right. It is not common to have a reverse curve in a tunnel. Also, the grade begins to drop in the tunnel, becoming 1.5% by the time you leave it. Portions of the tunnel have been reinforced with concrete. After leaving the tunnel, there are two short wood trestles that were filled in during the early 1900's. This is quite common on the line. When it was constructed, wood was plentiful and close to the track.

(48) *Locomotive 777 is at milepost 48, October 9, 2000.*

(Robert Royem Photo)

(49) *Looking west, the Cowee Tunnel is in the background. Note the water barrel on the bridge used for putting out fires from steam locomotive cinders. The bridge pier in the immediate foreground has been reworked and strengthened by Great Smoky Mountains Railroad.* *(R.D. Sharpless photo, Frank Ardrey collection)*

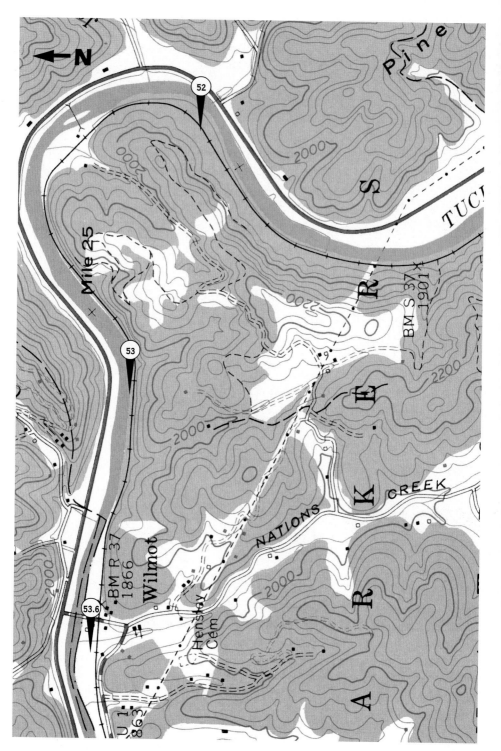

It was easy to construct a trestle over a ravine or low area. In time, however, trestles require a lot of maintenance, so track crews filled them in with dirt and cinders which were readily available and easy to transport once the railroad was built. At mile **49.7**, there is a flange lubricator. This is a device that applies a small amount of grease to the wheel flanges as the train passes by. The grease lubricates the flange of the rail to reduce friction between the rail and flange, making the wheels and rail last longer and providing a quieter ride for the passengers.

Wild turkeys are frequently seen in the area after the tunnel, especially in early summer.

50 Barker's Creek

For the first half mile, the line continues down at roughly a 1% grade. Barker's Creek is at mile **50.7**. There was once a sawmill here and a siding to serve it. The one-lane automobile bridge on the right is named the Jewel J. Revis bridge. He was Sarge Revis' father. Jewel became famous during a flood. The bridge washed out and he helped people get across the river. Rafting trips on the Tuckasegee River begin at Barker's Creek.

51 "S" Curves

This mile begins with a series of slight "s" curves, 3 to 5 degrees. The line actually climbs at 0.2% in this section. The last half of this mile ends with a gentle turn to the right.

52 Horseshoe curve #1

In the next mile, the train will totally reverse direction 180 degrees. The left curves are very gentle and it is not apparent without looking at the map that you are making the change. The grade descends the entire mile at 0.2%. At mile **52.4** there is a swinging footbridge across the river, closed in early 2000. Up to this point, the train speed has been limited to 10 miles per hour.

53 Wilmot

This mile continues with a descent at 0.2%. The community of Wilmot is at mile **53.5**. On the right is a large junkyard. One must remember that all rail travel is not beautiful countryside. The track crosses Nations Creek on a wood trestle.

(53.4) *Train being pulled by Steam engine No. 1702 approaching Wilmot at milepost **53.4** in September 2000.*
                                                            (Frank Strack photo)

*Train being pulled by Steam engine No. 1702 past Milepost **54** in September 2000.*
                                                            (Frank Strack photo)

54.7 *Steam engine No. 1702 passing the home of retired sheriff of Jackson County Fred Holcomb at milepost **54.7,** September 2000.* *(Frank Strack photo)*

Left and below: 1702 is headed west on October 9, 2000.
(Robert Royem Photo)

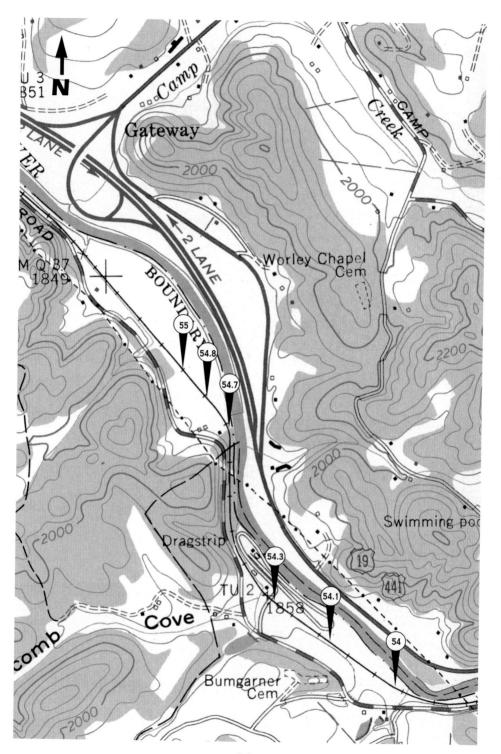

54 *Milepost 54, headed east toward Dillsboro.* (Michael George photo)

54 Old Racetrack

On the right, beginning at mile **54.1**, is the end of an old dragstrip. It is now a field with no trace of the racetrack. It was popular thirty-five years ago but was abandoned about 1970. The entrance to the dragstrip was at mile **54.3**, where there is now a trailer park. At mile **54.7**, retired sheriff Fred Holcomb lives on the left. He was sheriff of Jackson County for thirty years. At mile **54.9**, a half-mile long straight begins. Trains may travel up to 20 miles per hour here.

55 Strawberry and Tomato Fields

On the right side of the train you will see cultivated fields. Depending on the season, you might see strawberries or tomatoes planted. Thomas Valley Road is on the left.

56 Shelton Farms

This mile has another half-mile straight. The Shelton farm is a large farm with more tomatoes and strawberries.

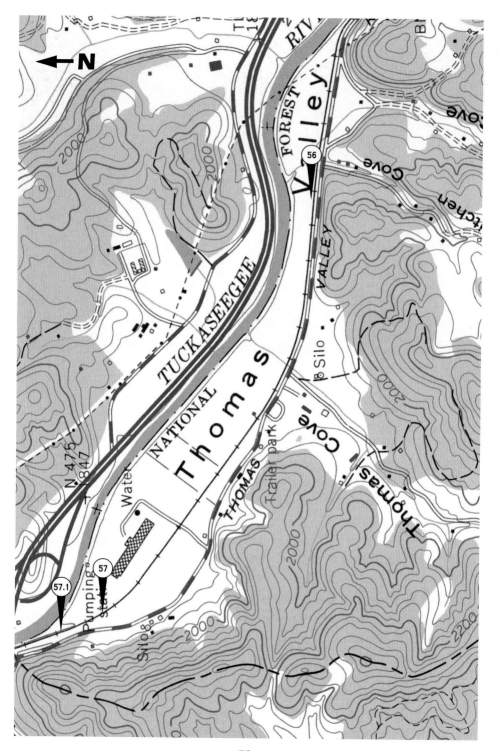

57 Whittier

At mile **57.1** there is a siding on the right that used to serve a furniture manufacturer. You may see some Great Smoky Mountains Railroad track maintenance equipment in the siding. At mile 57.2, the train will pass under highway 19/74 and then cross Connellys Creek on a ballasted deck wood trestle, 132 feet long. All other wood trestles on Great Smoky Mountains Railroad have an open deck. It is not known why this one trestle is different. At mile **57.4**, there is an old boarding house on the left. Whittier siding begins on the left. The depot was located near this end of the siding. In 1996, Jack Lemmon, James Garner, and Dan Akroyd were on board the Great Smoky Mountains Railroad during the making of the feature film, *My Fellow Americans*. The filming took place on this siding inside a huge blackout tent. At the road crossing, watch for another old boarding house on the right. It housed a barbershop also. At this point you will be travelling north. The Gourmet Dinner Train and Santa Express terminate their westward travel at Whittier and return to Dillsboro. The grade is still descending at 0.5%. As you leave the community the train enters a sharp 10 degree turn to the left. In this turn, on the left, is a house that dates from the late 1890's. This turn lasts for more than 90 degrees, so when you leave Whittier, you are now heading west again. Whittier was once in the heart of the old Cherokee Nation. The capitol was Stecoee. It was destroyed in 1776 when the Indians became allies with the British in the Revolutionary War. A little west of Whittier the train will pass the Cherokee Indian Reservation border, also known as the Qualla Boundary. The reservation is home to more than 8000 Cherokee and contains over 56,000 acres.

58 Tuckasegee River

This mile is full of slight "s" curves and is very close to the Tuckasegee River. At mile **58.6**, watch for an old house on the left. This mile ends with a 12 degree left turn.

59 Ela

Watch the river on the right side and you will see a beautiful cascading rapid. This right turn is also 12 degrees. At mile **59.5**, the Oconaluftee River flows into the Tuckasegee. This river comes from Cherokee. At mile **59.9**, you will pass through the community of Ela. In the early 1900's, this was a bustling community. Another railroad interchanged here, the Appalachian Railway. It was a logging line that brought timber to a sawmill here. As the train enters the 5 degree left turn, you are at the point where the

Appalachian Railway crossed the Tuckasegee River. However, it will not be visible from the train. There was also a depot, but it was torn down by the late forties and replaced with a whistle stop shed.

(57.4) *Left: Steam engine 1702 headed west coming into Whittier in September 2000. Bottom: Steam locomotive 1702 passing in front one of the old boarding houses in Whittier.*
(Frank Strack photos)

(57.5) *Old boarding house in Whitter that was believed to have had a barbershop in it. A lot of shrubbery hides the front of the building.* *(Frank Strack photo)*

(57.7) *Old house that dates back to the late 1890's.* *(Frank Strack photo)*

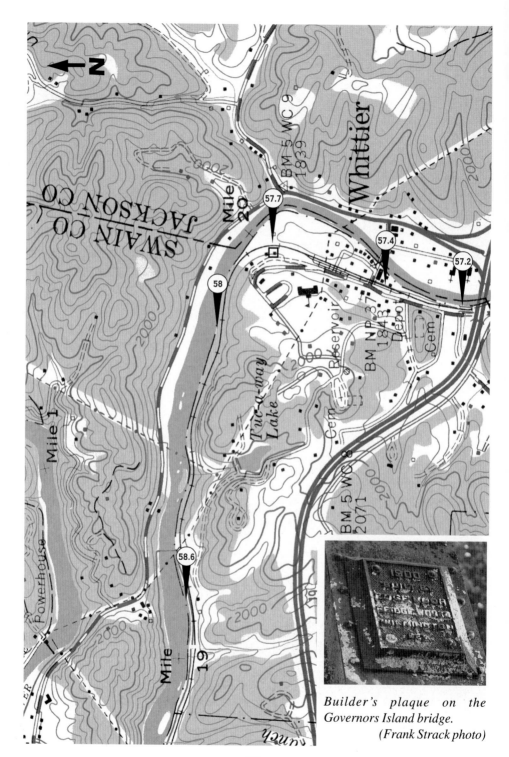

N

SWAIN CO
JACKSON CO

Whittier

BM 5 WC 9
1839

Mile 20

57.7

57.4

57.2

BM NP 37
1843

Depot

Reservoir

Cem

Cem

Cem

Tuc-a-way
Lake

58

2000

Mile 1

Powerhouse

BM 5 WC 8
2071

2000

58.6

2000

Mile 19

Builder's plaque on the
Governors Island bridge.
(Frank Strack photo)

62

60.5 *This crossing of the Tuckasegee River is 652.5 ft. long. The 132 ft. long truss was built in 1900. The bank on the left is the one that has been reinforced with junk cars.*

(Michael George photo)

60.5 *Train 17 is westbound crossing the Tuckasegee River at Governors Island on 5-23-47. The gentleman sitting on the porch has an excellent location for train-watching.*

(R.D. Sharpless photo, Frank Ardrey collection).

The Wavers

Train riders are occasionally in for a big surprise on the ride between Dillsboro and Bryson City. A couple from Greenville, South Carolina, comes up several times a summer. They station themselves at the Huddle House in Dillsboro and wave as the train leaves town. Then, they get into their car and drive a short distance to place themselves in front of the train. They hop out of their car and pick up some walking sticks and wave, looking like they are hikers. After another frantic drive to get ahead of the train, they again park and place themselves beside a creek and hold a pair of children's fishing poles. Of course,

they wave at the passengers. By this time, some train riders have figured out that something unusual is going on. They continue to chase the train and get ahead of it all the way to Bryson City. At some points, they will appear to be playing checkers on the hood of their car. Or, they may spread out a checkered tablecloth and look like they are picnicking. Sometimes, they set up a "fake" yard sale advertising items at 75% off everything, knowing there is no way the passengers can get off the train to purchase anything!

Sometimes they hold up a sign saying "Happy Birthday" or "Happy Trains." The odds are pretty high that someone riding the

The Proctors pose looking like the farmers in the American Gothic painting.
(Frank Strack photos both pages)

train will have a birthday. The last, most dramatic act from the wavers is an attack on the train with "Supersoaker" water guns. They shoot at the passengers and crew alike. It is all great fun for everyone involved.

As the train arrives in Bryson City, the wavers wait for the passengers to detrain. Then, they hand out articles about themselves, talk to the passengers, and invite them to sign a "guest book."

Who are the wavers? They are Jack and Betty Proctor. Jack is a cabinetmaker and Betty is a homemaker. They are not paid to do what they do for the railroad passengers. It is a two-hour drive one way for them to come up from Greenville, and they do it all for the enjoyment of seeing smiling passengers.

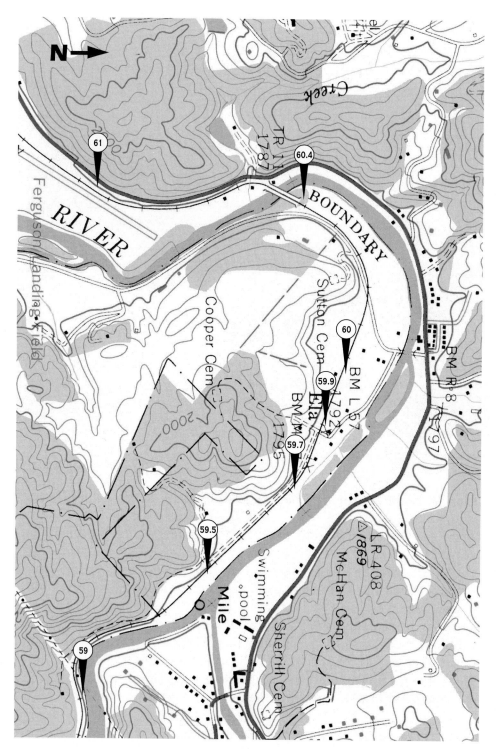

N →

Creek

TR 11
1787

61

60.4

Ferguson Landing Field

RIVER

BOUNDARY

Sutton Cem

Cooper Cem

2000

60

BM L 57
1792

59.9

Ela

BM M
1795

59.7

BM R 8
1797

59.5

Mile

Swimming
pool

LR 408
△ 1869
McHan Cem

Sherrill Cem

59

60 Tuckasegee River Crossing

After leaving Ela, the train makes another left turn. There is a grade crossing with Highway 19 at mile **60.2**. The Tuckasegee River crossing is at mile **60.5**. The first part of the crossing is made on a wood trestle. Then there are four thirty-foot-long steel deck plate girder bridges. The truss bridge is 132 feet long and was built in 1900. The next section of bridge is a 56-foot long deck plate girder, followed by another section of wood trestle. The total length of the bridge is 652.5 feet. After leaving the truss bridge, the remaining portion of the bridge curves left at 13 degrees. Highway 19 is on the right. At some point many years ago, it was decided to reinforce the bank between the river and the highway with old junk cars. In the winter these old cars are visible on the right bank of the river. A study is underway to determine a more ecologically sound method of holding the bank.

61 Governors Island/Ferguson Field

Ferguson Field is the name of a grass landing strip that used to be at mile **61.1**. A portion of it is now used for radio-controlled model airplanes. Behind the airstrip, there is a grassy mound in the field. It is a ceremonial mound used by the Cherokee Indians, one of six known to exist in the area. The Cherokee name for the 1000-year-old community was Keetawa. Originally, the mound was probably 30 feet high. It is now only about four feet high. There is an unused dairy farm on both sides of the track at mile **61.5**. This was once the largest dairy farm in Western North Carolina. There is a short 1.8% climbing grade to mile **61.6**. The track then descends again. Watch for rabbits beside the track at mile 61.6. There seems to be a large population of them here.

62 Scary Branch

The railroad crosses Scary Branch at mile **62.8**. There is a steep winding road climbing the mountain. Supposedly, some houses at the end of the road had some scary things about them, giving the road and creek its name. Watch for a cave in the right turn at mile **62.9**. It is a little above eye level.

63 Bryson City

New road crossing signals have been installed at mile **63.4**. The track

62.8 *Steam engine 1702 headed into Bryson City along the Tuckasegee River.*

(Frank Strack photo)

60.5 *Steam engine 1702 is on the Tuck-asegee River bridge at Governors Island near Bryson City.*

(Frank Strack photos)

(61) *Steam engine 1702 headed west at Ferguson Landing Field.*   *(Frank Strack photo)*

(61.1) *Cherokee Burial mound at the Ferguson Landing Field.*   *(Frank Strack photo)*

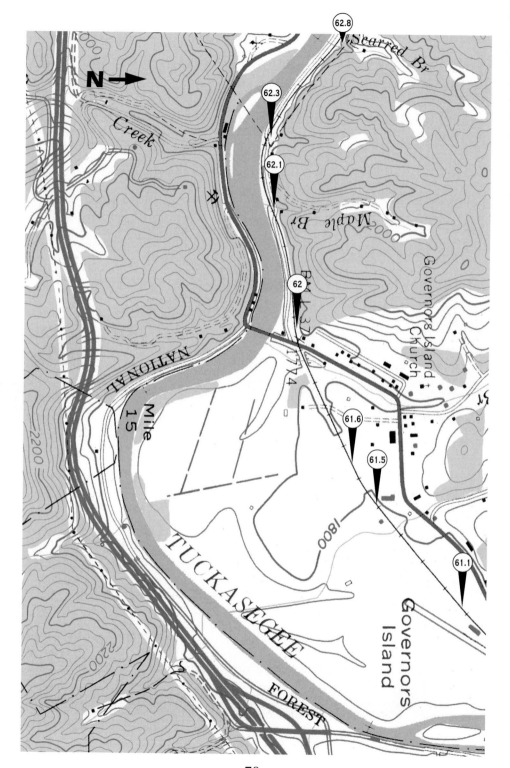

63.5 *Deep Creek crossing.* *(Michael George photo)*

then crosses Deep Creek on steel deck girder bridges, 107 feet long. The bridges are in a left curve of 3.6 degrees. Deep Creek is popular for tubing. It originates not far from Newfound Gap on the Tennessee/North Carolina border. At mile **63.5**, the track begins to descend at 0.5%. Mile **63.7** is the east end of the Bryson City siding. Usually there will be two tank cars in this siding, a large one for fueling the diesel locomotives and a smaller one containing bunker oil for the steam engine. On the right, watch for the old Standard Oil Company tanks, no longer in use. The depot, dating from the 1890's, is at mile **63.9**. It is the only depot on Great Smoky Mountains Railroad that survived from the time Southern Railway owned the line. Southern Railway removed the freight storage end of the depot. Great Smoky Mountains Railroad has added an open portico for passengers to sit in. The building in the corner of the railroad and Everett Street opposite the depot was the Entella Hotel. Numerous food and gift shops are in the area close to the depot. Bryson City was originally called "Big Bear Springs" by the Cherokee.

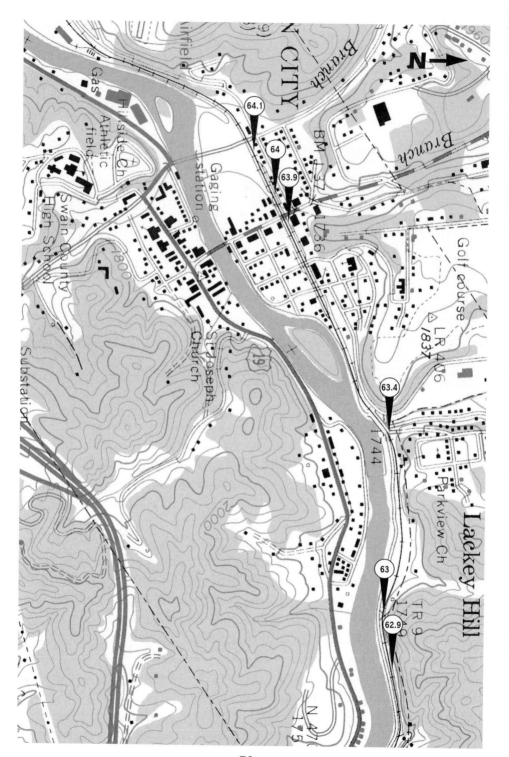

(63.9) *Bryson City Depot in July 2000.*   *(Frank Strack photo)*

(63.9) *Bryson City Depot in 1984.*   *(Michael George photo)*

(64.8) *Train 17, pulled by Ps-2 #1256 on May 23, 1947, is crossing the Tuckasegee River on the old Nantahala #2 truss bridge, moved to this location and strengthened during the* Fontana relocation.   *(R.D. Sharpless photo, Frank Ardrey collection)*

64 Tuckasegee River Crossing

For a time, it was just called Bryson, and before that it was called Charleston. Now, on a fall weekend when the colors are at their prettiest, one might think Bryson City was about as busy as it could get. There was a time, however, when no rooms were available in town for a few *years*. Bryson City is the closest town to Fontana Dam, and during its construction it was absolutely covered with TVA employees, contractors, and railroaders. During this time, railroaders would try to avoid work on the Murphy Branch, because instead of spending the night in a room, they would be stuck sleeping on the caboose. During the days of steam locomotives, facilities in Bryson included a water tank, coal chute, and in early days a turntable. This was replaced with a wye located on the west end of town. It was later moved closer to the depot, about where the Southern Concrete Company is today. The coal chute had a steep track going to it where coal was loaded in buckets that held about a ton each. Watch closely on the right at Milepost 64 and you will see the old coal dock in the weeds. Ashes were dumped and grates cleaned in Bryson also. In steam days, one locomotive was assigned full time to Bryson City.

Several industries were located in Bryson City. Some of them were the

74

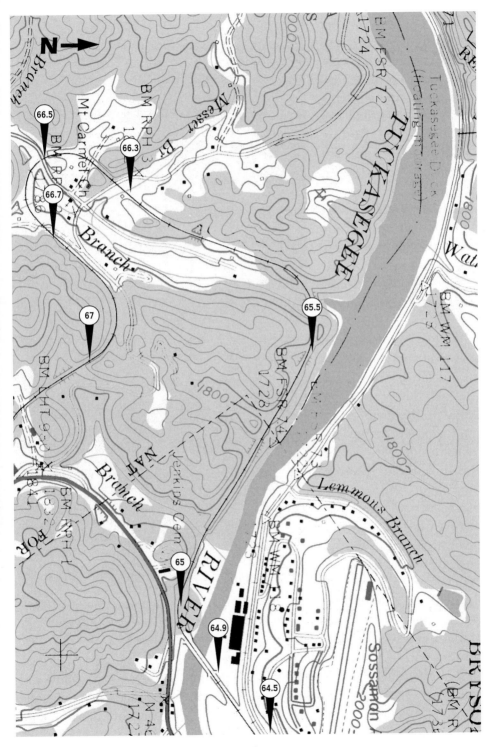

75

Carolina Wood Turning Company, the concrete plant, a petroleum dealer, a pulpwood loading area, Carolina Building Supply and a coal dealership. The Carolina Wood Turning Company made furniture. Bryson was considered a yard on the timetable. It stretched for a mile and a half, but was only four tracks wide at the widest point, and none of the tracks were very long. Many of the tracks served the industries. During the Fontana Dam construction so many cars of cement came into town that they would have to be stored on the mainline at times. The wye for turning steam locomotives was on the left. Great Smoky Mountains Railroad has purchased a turntable and plans to install it so the steam locomotive can be turned. At mile **64.5**, the original roadbed curved to the right and followed the north bank of the Tuckasegee River. The

(63.9) *P-1 4-6-2 No. 1288 is at Bryson City circa 1946. Noti* *climbing down the ladder. Also notice express boxcar in f* *today.*

construction of Fontana Dam would have flooded the line west of Bryson City, so the route had to be relocated. The route your train will follow was built in 1944. The river crossing is at mile **64.9**. This bridge was completely fabricated from used components. Since the relocation was done during World

*n crew: the engineer oiling the running gear, the conductor in his black suit, and the fireman
station platform. These cars were to carry less-than-carload freight, similar to what U.P.S. does*
(Photo from collection of Dale Roberts)

War II, no new steel could be used on railroad construction. The truss bridge
on this 426 foot crossing came from another crossing of the Nantahala River
that would be flooded in the relocation. The bridge was originally built in
1898.

65 Relocated Line

After crossing the bridge, the track curves to the right at 12.1 degrees. The train is now on the relocated mainline. You should notice a change in the way the railroad looks. Previously, cuts through rock were made by hand, so cuts were only wide enough to let the train pass. Remember, all of the roadbed prior to mile 65 was done by men with hand tools. In 1944, no new steel could be used, but modern grading equipment was available to make deep cuts and large fills. Bulldozers, dump trucks, and other large earth-moving equipment were used. Thus, the roadbed is more "open" and you will begin to see large amounts of Kudzu, used to stabilize the large cuts and fills. The line begins climbing at 1.3%. Since loaded trains generally moved east on the railroad, the relocation was designed so eastbound trains would have the least amount of grade. Westbound, the grade was steeper. At mile **65.5**, the train will make an 8.1 degree curve to the left, changing direction more than 90 degrees.

66 2nd Horseshoe Curve

At Milepost 66, there is a railcar on the left. It is not from an accident but was intentionally placed there by the landowner. At mile **66.3**, the horseshoe curve begins. It is a 12 degree curve to the left. When there aren't leaves on the trees, the track will be visible across the valley to your left where the train will shortly be travelling in the opposite direction. At mile **66.5**, new crossing gates have been installed on Robinson Gap Road. At mile 66.7, look to your left again and you may see the track you were just on moments before. In the middle of the 10.2 degree curve to the right the train will be pointed toward the Tuckasegee River bridge you crossed a few moments ago.

67

The climbing grade reduces to 0.4% in this mile. Note the large amount of Kudzu. At mile **67.9**, Highway 19 will be visible on the left.

68 Jackson Line Gap

The summit of the climb from Bryson City is reached at mile **68.7** in Jackson Line Gap. The grade now begins to descend at 0.6%. There was a passing siding that began here, called Brooks siding.

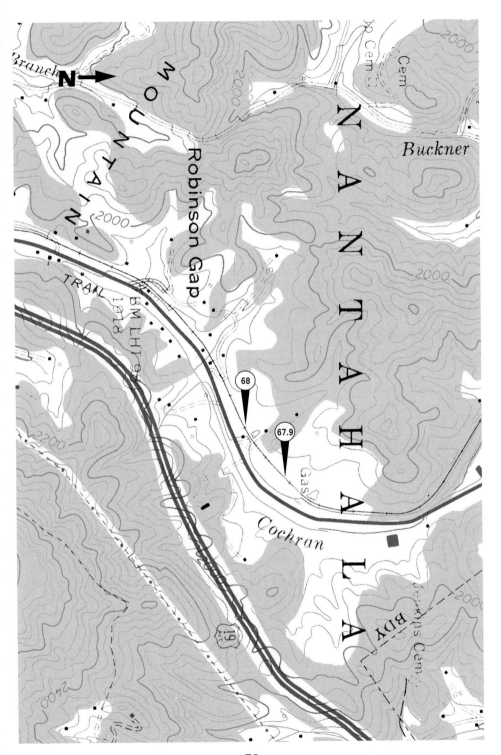

71.6 *The finishing touches are being placed on the bridge at milepost 71.6 on the relocated line, June 28, 1944.* *(TVA photo, courtesy of Federal Records Center)*

69 Large Fill

Note the very large fill at mile **69.3**. It took an incredible amount of material to make this fill. Keep in mind that some fills on the relocated track are over 100 feet high. Alarka creek is visible on the left at mile **69.6**. Notice the interesting concrete highway bridge over the creek. Mile **69.8** will find you on another large fill. Look for the old farmhouse on the right.

70 Sam Davis Road Crossing

At mile **70.5**, the track crosses Sam Davis Road. The angle of the crossing between the railroad and road is such that a very long gate arm, 36 feet long, was required when the gates were installed. Watch for wild turkeys in this section of track.

71 Overpass

The grade is now descending at 0.9%. At mile **71.6**, there is a 10.5 degree curve to the right. In the middle of the curve is a road overpass on a wood trestle. The road is also in a curve, making for a very dangerous area for an automobile driver. It has been said that the engineer in charge of building the bridge said "I've done all I can do. It's in God's hands now."

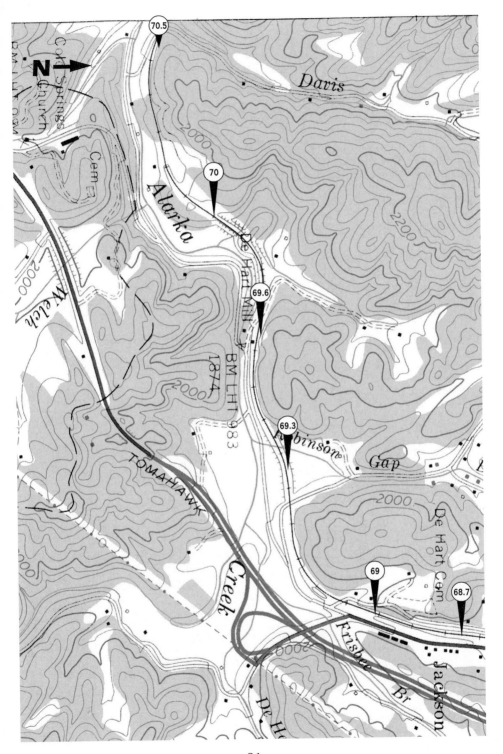

81

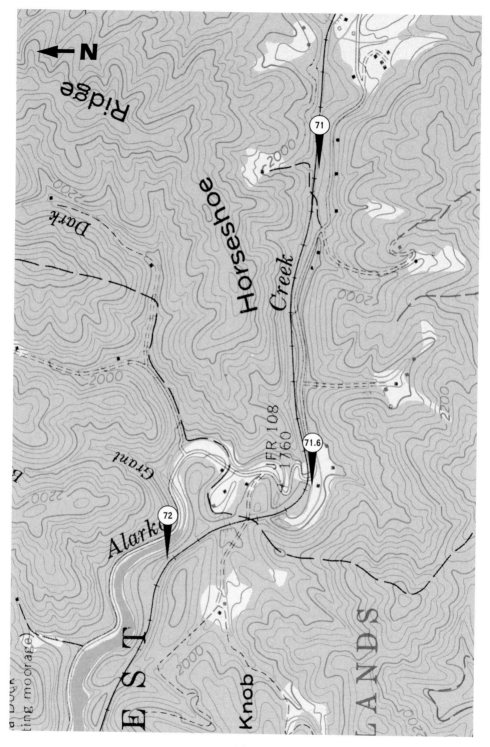

82

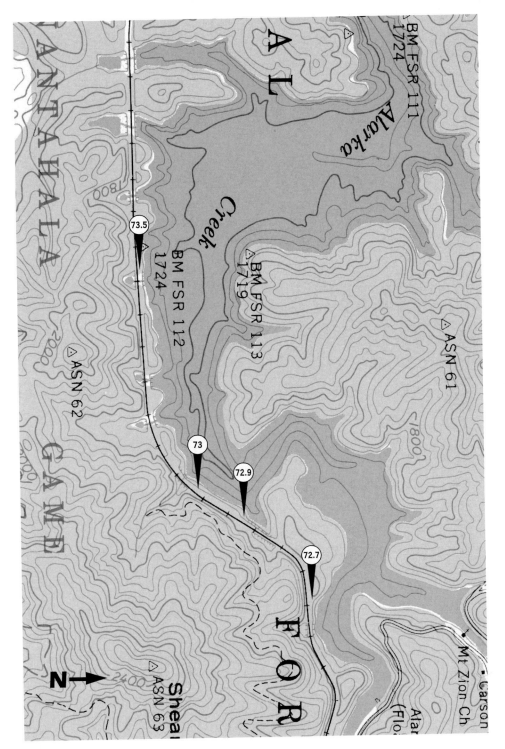

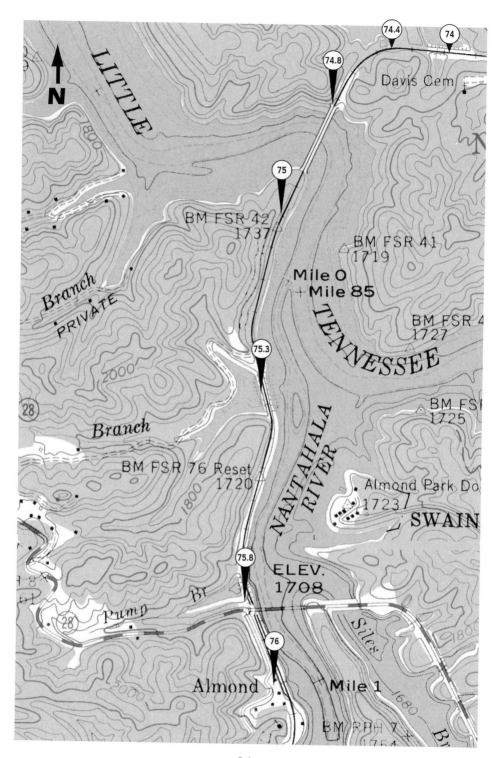

N

LITTLE

74.4
74
Davis Cem

74.8

75

BM FSR 42
1737

BM FSR 41
1719

Mile 0
Mile 85

Branch
PRIVATE

TENNESSEE

BM FSR 4
1727

2000

75.3

BM FSR
1725

28

Branch

NANTAHALA RIVER

BM FSR 76 Reset
1720

Almond Park Do
1723

SWAIN

1800

75.8

ELEV.
1708

28

Pump

Br

Siles

76

Almond

Mile 1

BM RBH 7
1754

Legend has it that no two cars have ever met under the bridge. You won't be able to see it, but as you come out of this curve there is a large concrete arch bridge, 26 x 25 feet by 172 feet long under a 75-foot-high fill. The bridge spans Alarka Creek.

72 Fontana Lake

The first view of Fontana Lake is on the right at mile **72.2**. Depending on the amount of foliage on the trees and the level of water in the lake, you may not be able to see the lake yet. The speed limit on trains at this point is 20 mph. By mile **72.7**, Fontana Lake should be easily seen out the right side of the train.

73 Bear Crossing

In 1997/98, there was not a lot of "mast" or food for animals in the Great Smoky Mountains. Wildlife had to go outside the park to find food. Many bears were seen in this area during that time period. Near the end of this mile, the descending grade ends and the track climbs briefly at 0.3%. McLain Siding was located in the straight section. It is hard to imagine, but where the lake is to the right was once a fertile farm valley full of crops.

74 Fontana Lake Crossing

Near the end of the straight, the track begins to descend again at 0.5%. After making an 8.3% curve to the left, the 777-foot-long Fontana Lake Bridge will come into view. The bridge is at mile **74.8**. See Chapter 3 for more details about the construction of this bridge. Portions of the movie *Forces of Nature*, starring Sandra Bullock and Ben Afleck, were filmed on this bridge.

75 Almond Depot

Extensive grading and filling were required in this section of the relocated mainline. At mile **75.4** the train will be on the Turkey Creek fill. This huge fill spans an entire valley. See Chapter 3 for more details. Almond Boat Park is on the left at mile **75.7**. During the relocation, a new depot for Almond was built at mile **75.9**. There was a passing siding on the right in front of the depot and another single-ended siding was on the left. Almond is an interesting little community.

74.6 *The Little Tennessee crossing of Fontana Lake at low water on a crystal clear winter day in 1985.* *(Michael George photo)*

This is what the old community of Almond looks like today at low water. The roadbed of the old line is visible along with the piers for the Nantahala River crossing. The Little Tennessee River crossing used by Great Smoky Mountains Railroad is in the distance.

(Michael George photo)

76 Brosnan Summer Home

On the left is former Southern Railway President D.W. Brosnan's summer home. The house itself is not visible, but the remnants of a huge orchard may be seen along the left side of the track. Large meetings for Southern Railway management were held here, and solid trains of office cars filled the sidings. It has been said that Mr. Brosnan would occasionally fire employees at these meetings. They would not be allowed to ride the train away from Almond and had to provide their own transportation. This was not an easy task from such a remote location as Almond. A small siding was located on the left after the right curve past the milepost.

77 Sharp Curve

Beginning at mile **75.5**, the grade has been level. It will remain that way until mile 78. The sharpest curve on the relocation is at mile **77.8**. This right curve is 14.2 degrees. Trains are limited to 5 miles per hour through the curve. The Nantahala River makes a 125 degree bend at this location.

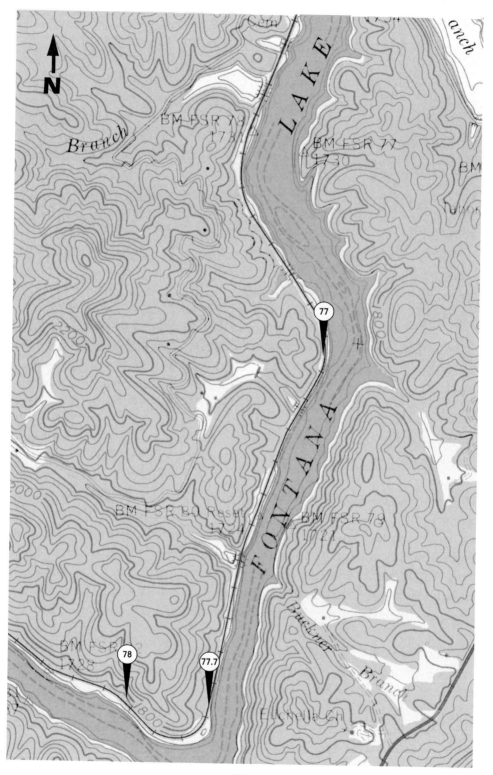

Site of the old Nantahala #2 truss bridge. At low water, the east abutment and the pier for the west end of the bridge are visible. *(Michael George photo)*

78 Old Nantahala No. 2.

At mile **78.7** the bridge abutments for the old Nantahala No. 2 truss bridge may be seen when the water level is low in the lake.

(79.9) *Steam engine 1702 at Nantahala Outdoor Whitewater Rafting Center in Wesser on July 2000.* *(Frank Strack photo)*

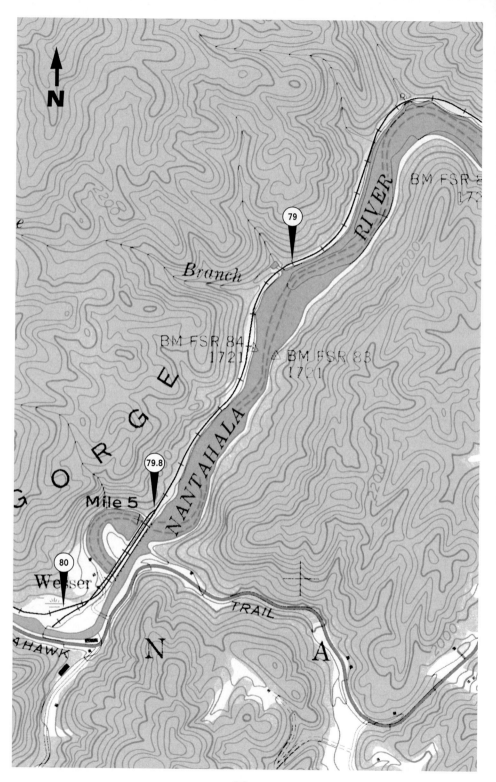

(79.9) *Steam engine 1702 waiting for the return trip to Bryson City at Wesser.*
(Michael George photo)

79 Wesser

Mile 79 is the last mile of relocated track. Watch for Wesser Creek Falls on the left at mile **79.8**. These falls were created by TVA during the relocation. The river channel was straightened here to eliminate two long bridges. The old river channel is on the right and goes behind a ridge. At mile **79.9** a new double ended siding has been installed by Great Smoky Mountains Railroad. This siding was necessary when excursions from Andrews needed to pass the Nantahala Gorge excursion. Wesser is the eastern terminus for trips from Andrews. Bryson City trains continue to Nantahala, then reverse and layover in Wesser for an hour. The Nantahala Outdoor Center is located here, center for many outdoor activities.

80 Appalachian Trail

Great Smoky Mountains Railroad begins following the Nantahala River at Almond. There are mountains around, but upon leaving Wesser, there is no doubt that one is in the Nantahala Gorge. In the Cherokee language, Nantahala means "land of the noonday sun." It was given this name because the sun only shines into the gorge during the middle hours of the day since the mountains are so steep and rise so high around it. Up to this point, traveling on the railroad is interesting, but there is something about entering the gorge that makes it unique and special. Highway 19 is on one side of the river and the railroad is on the other. The railroad is in view most of the time from the highway. In many places it seems like there isn't enough room for the track to pass between the water and steep mountainside. The vegetation is lush and grows close to the track. The air is cool and fresh.

Whitewater rafters, kayakers, and canoeists enjoy this river every month of the year. The Appalachian Trail crosses the railroad at Wesser at Milepost 80. Things change at this point, and it is obvious that you are back on a railroad carved out of the mountainside with pick and shovel instead of dynamite and bulldozer. The grade begins to climb at 0.4%.

(79.9) *Photo taken from the Appalachian Trail on a crystal clear winter day in 1985.*
(Michael George photo)

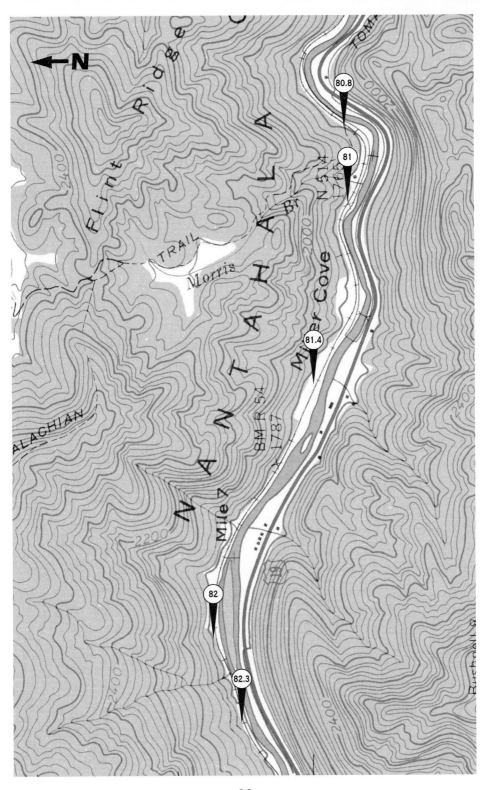

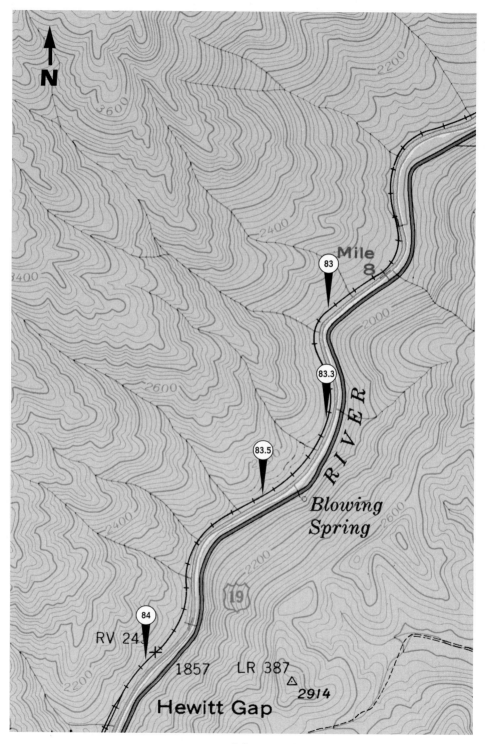

Train 17 is west of Wesser along the Nantahala River. The date is May 23, 1947. Ps-2 #1256 was one of only four engines of this class to operate on the Murphy Branch.
(R.D. Sharpless photo, Frank Ardrey collection)

GP-7 #2191 is eastbound between Talc Mountain and Wesser in May, 1954. Note the loaded wood rack cars bound for Canton.   (R.D. Sharpless photo, Frank Ardrey collection)

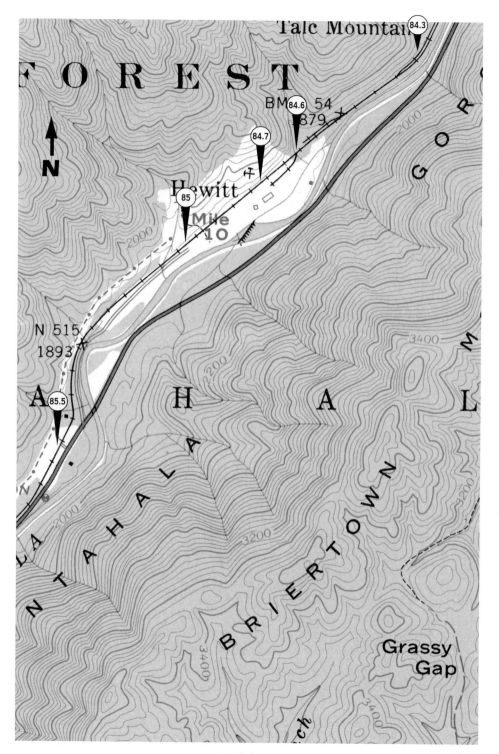

81 Caves

Watch on the right at mile **81.4** for some caves, set back from the track and a little higher than the train windows. Legend has it that the Cherokees used these caves during the Trail of Tears. Relics have been found in them. They are also said to have been used by slaves, hunters, and settlers.

This area is quite memorable for the railroaders that worked here, but not because of the caves. They remember something very dangerous in this area: snakes. Close to the quarry, copperheads and rattlesnakes were numerous. One might wonder why someone on a train would be concerned about snakes. When switching cars, the brakeman has to get off the train to throw the switch. Much of the switching takes place at night. Nighttime is when copperheads and rattlesnakes come out in the summer. And what better place for a snake on a cool autumn evening than the warm ballast and ties that have been soaking up the sun all day? Pity the poor brakeman that steps on one while walking the track. Those stainless steel signaling lamps don't put out much light.

(83.3) *Monument to kayaker.*   *(Frank Strack photo)*

82 Miller Cove

There is an island in the Nantahala River at Milepost 82. At one time there was a house on the right side of the track. Partons Bridge is on the left at mile **82.4**. At mile **82.8**, a 5.5 degree curve turn precedes a 14.2 degree right curve.

83 Talc Mountain

The sharpest curve on Great Smoky Mountains Railroad is at mile **83.2**. It is a 17 degree curve to the left. At mile **83.3**, there is a monument on the left dedicated to a kayaker who drowned in the river. At mile

86.7 *Westbound consolidation Ks-1 #848 with baggage car taking on coal at Nantahala in Ja*

83.5, there was a short siding on the right. It served the North Carolina Talc and Mining Company, no longer in existence. At mile **83.7**, a 24-foot-long trestle was filled in.

84 Hewitt

It is not known how this community got its name, but high up on the mountain to your left, there is a location called "Hewitts Gap." At mile **84.5**,

. Depot is in background on right. (Photo from Dale Roberts collection, courtesy of Jim King)

there was a short siding on the right, now covered with material from the rock quarry. At mile **84.6**, there is still a siding to serve the rock quarry. Little rock is shipped by rail, though, and Great Smoky Mountains Railroad uses the siding to store maintenance of way equipment.

85

A 36-foot-long trestle has been filled in at mile **85.3**. The highway is

83.3 *No. 1288 is taking on coal at Nantahala circa 1946.*

now between the railroad and the river. At mile **85.4**, there is a 12.9 degree right curve. At one time there was a short (288 feet) siding on the right at mile **85.5**.

86 Nantahala

There used to be a water tank for filling steam locomotive tenders at

(Photo from collection of Dale Robert)

Milepost 86. At mile **86.1**, the Stanley track begins on the right. This track is used to make a "runaround" at the end of the trip. The locomotive uncouples from the train, moves past the switch, backs through the side track, and then couples to the opposite end of the train. This way the locomotive is on the front of the train for the return trip. During steam locomotive days, Nantahala had enough importance to require "yard limit" signs at each end. There was an engine servicing area that consisted of a water tank, coal chute, and sand tower. For many years, this was the last opportunity to load coal on the Murphy Branch. Trains were required to make it to Murphy and back on one full tender of coal. It is twenty-eight hard miles from Nantahala to Murphy, including three miles of Red Marble grade. This load had to keep the engine under steam all night at Murphy, too. Towards the end of steam, a coal chute was installed in Murphy to make it a little easier on the fireman. The depot was across the track from the coal chute and sand tower at mile **86.6**. There is now a large patch of tall weeds where the depot stood.

In 1975, the Graham County Railroad ceased operations after two of its bridges were washed out in a heavy rain. The Burlington Industries furni-

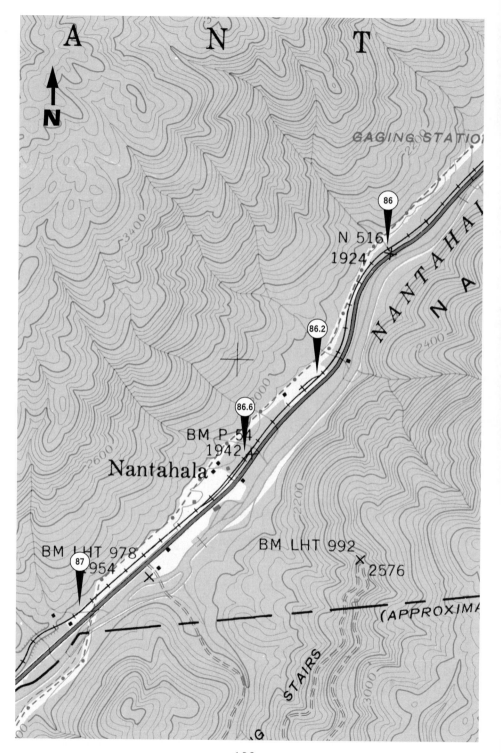

ture factory could no longer ship its freight by train from Robbinsville to Topton. The furniture was then trucked to a siding in Nantahala and loaded in boxcars. There was a structure that looked similar to a coal tower at the east end of the yard near this siding. This was used to store salt for highway use in the winter. It was torn down in the 1980's.

87 Red Marble Grade

Red Marble Grade will comprise the next three miles. Without a doubt, this is the steepest part of Great Smoky Mountains Railroad. In these three miles the railroad will climb 600 feet. The average grade for these three miles is 5.8%. In places it exceeds 6%. In the steam era, it would take two locomotives on the front of a train and a third one pushing on the rear to get a train of 8 or 10 cars up the mountain. The third locomotive came from Andrews and waited in the siding at Nantahala to assist the westbound train. Today, one of Great Smoky Mountains Railroad's diesel locomotives can only take three loaded grain cars up the grade. Southern Railway used 85 pound rail on the Murphy Branch. All of mile 87 has had 100 pound rail installed by Great Smoky Mountains Railroad. Near the end of this mile, there is a 12 degree curve to the left.

(87.5) *Southern Railway caboose X667 is descending Red Marble grade behind a short train in February of 1983.* *(Michael George photo)*

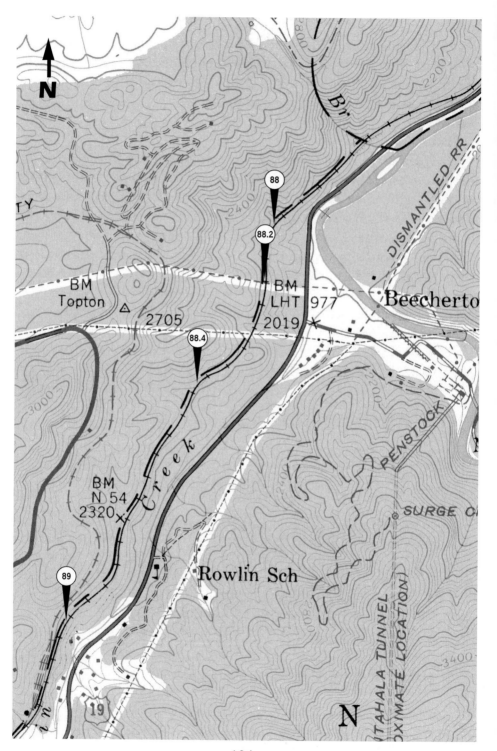

N

88

88.2

BM
Topton

BM
LHT 977

Beecherto

2705

2019

88.4

BM
N 54
2320

Creek

3000

PENSTOCK

SURGE C

Rowlin Sch

89

19

N

NANTAHALA TUNNEL
(APPROXIMATE LOCATION)

DISMANTLED RR

88 Grave of Jane Downs

About 100 feet to the left, down the slope, is a grave at mile **88.2**. The marker says "Jane Downs, bride of WM. H. Deaver, killed in 1852 when lean to fell in on Winding Stairs Road." That is all that is known about this mysterious gravesite high on the mountainside. A 112-foot-long trestle was filled in at mile 88.4.

(87.5)

(Frank Strack photo)

89 Graham County Railroad Interchange

The Graham County Railroad was the last logging line to interchange with the Southern Railway. It went from this location to Robbinsville. The Graham County used Shays for locomotives. The Shay would bring its train to the interchange and wait for the Southern Railway train to climb the grade and exchange cars. There are photos of shiny black and white Southern diesels sitting next to the old worn out Shays in the three track interchange yard. Interestingly, old railroaders say that the Shay would sometimes assist the Southern train by pushing on the rear to Topton. This of course is "unofficial" information, since the rule book would not allow such a thing. Watch for a stone wall on the right. The three-track yard was above the wall. The tracks have all been removed. The Graham County lasted until 1975 when several bridges were washed out. Bears have been seen here by Great Smoky Mountains Railroad crews. Mile **89.6** is the location of Hawks Nest Trestle, 400 feet long and 43 feet high. It was filled in during the 1940's. The curve alignment was altered also to reduce sharp curvature at the west side of the trestle. In the winter when there is no vegetation, you might see a trestle bent sticking out of the dirt on the left side. When the trestle was filled in, the track was moved slightly to the right.

105

(87.5) *Graham County Railroad interchange tracks. Top: east end of yard. Bottom: looking west from east end. Photo taken in February of 1983. (Michael George photo)*

Opposite page bottom: Ps-2 #1256 is westbound to Murphy on train 17 climbing Red Marble grade on May 23, 1947. It is crossing the filled-in Hawks Nest trestle. Someone is sitting in the open Railway Post Office door, no doubt enjoying the view and the sound of 1256 struggling up the nearly five percent grade. It appears that 1256 has taken on a full load of coal at Nantahala.   *(R.D. Sharpless photo, Frank Ardrey collection)*

106

Andrews switcher Ks-2 #735 is pushing train #68, the Blue Goose, up Red Marble grade, westbound to Topton, 1946. Brakeman can be seen riding boxcar in front of caboose. Photo taken from tender of lead engine.   (Frank Clodfelter photo, J.T. Earwood collection)

The Andrews switcher, Ks-2 #695, is backing down Red Marble grade with caboose X2187 on May 23, 1947. *(R.D. Sharpless photo, Frank Ardrey collection)*

This portion of the Hawks Nest Trestle was still visible in July 2000.
(Linton Brooks photo)

(89.6) *Hawks Nest fill in July 2000.* (Michael George photo)

(87.5) *Green and white Southern Railway GP-7 #2191 is eastbound at Nantahala in May, 1954. The train has just descended Red Marble grade. Highway 19 is on the left and the cleared area above the telegraph pole is Red Marble grade just west of the Graham County Railroad interchange and the filled in Hawks Nest trestle.*

(R.D. Sharpless photo, Frank Ardrey collection)

90.6 *Great Smoky Mountains Railroad Highrailer at Topton.* *(Frank Strack photo)*

90 Topton

Topton is the top of the grade. It is downhill for the next 10 miles, all the way to Andrews. The grade going west drops sharply, but it is not as steep as Red Marble, descending four hundred feet in the next three miles. Freight trains doubling the hill used two tracks at Topton for storing cars. Cars would also be brought by the Andrews switcher and left in the siding for the eastbound freight. It is a requirement to stop at Topton and turn up retainers on the freight and passenger cars. This procedure changes the operation of the air brakes. The brake cylinder will maintain pressure on the braking system while allowing the reservoir on each car to recharge with air. This is something that is normally done on steep grades on all railroads. The descending grade is 3.9%. The railroad begins following a new river at this point, the Valley River. It is to your right, but at this point is little more than a creek. There are ten crossings of this river between here and Andrews.

91 Valley River Crossing

There is a filled in trestle at Milepost 91. It was only 16 feet long. At mile **91.2**, the Valley River is crossed. Great Smoky Mountains Railroad

110

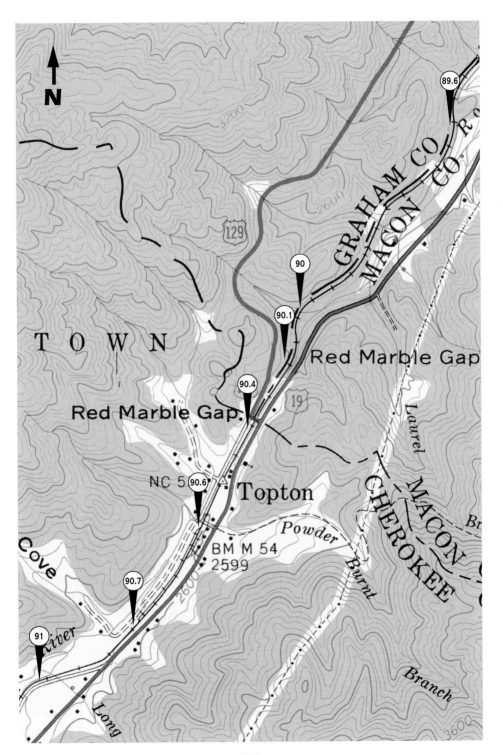

N

89.6

GRAHAM CO.
MACON CO.

129

90

90.1

Red Marble Gap

TOWN

90.4

Red Marble Gap.

19

Laurel

NC 5 90.6

Topton

MACON
CHEROKEE

Powder

Cove

Burnt

BM M 54
2599

90.7

Br

River

91

Long

Branch

111

has reinforced the embankment with rock. At mile **91.8**, the Valley River is crossed again. It is now back on the right side of the train. A junkyard on the right will be visible at mile **91.9**. The land owner became angry when the railroad made claim to its 50 foot right of way and piled cars as high as possible right next to the track. The grade has reduced to 2.5% by the end of this mile.

92

The descending grade increases to 3.2% in this mile. At mile **92.4**, there is an 11 degree curve to the right. At mile **92.6**, there is a trestle over the Valley River and a driveway. The Valley River is now back on the left.

93 Rhodo/Site of Passenger Train Wreck

At Milepost 93, there is a trestle. At mile **93.1** on April 17, 1941, Southern Railway passenger train No. 17 entered this curve at a speed in excess of 50 miles per hour and the locomotive and tender left the track and turned over in a creek. The engineer and fireman were killed. At mile **93.6**, the Valley River is crossed again. At mile **93.9** the smallest trestle on the Great

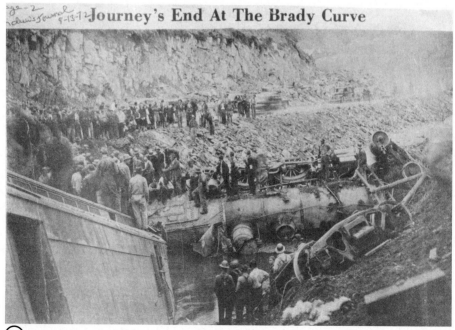

Journey's End At The Brady Curve

(93.1) *See story on page 115.*   *(Andrews Journal 9-13-72, collection of Jim King)*

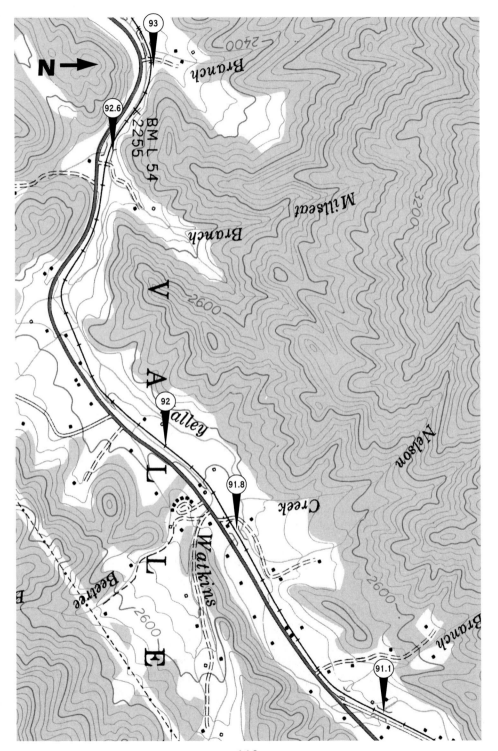

N →

93

92.6

BM L 54
× 2255

Branch

Branch

Millseat

2400

3200

2600

V

A

L

L

E

Beetree

alley

Watkins

Creek

Nelson

Branch

92

91.8

91.1

2600

2600

113

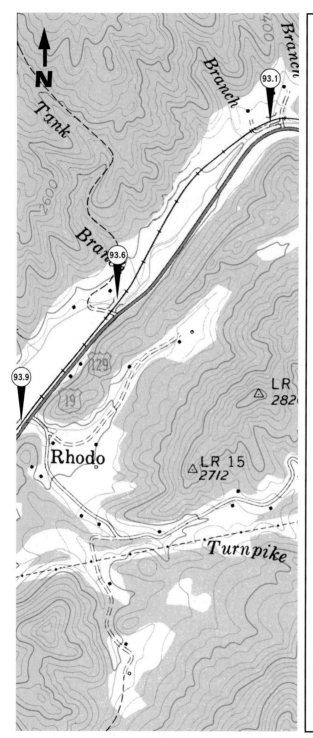

*Opposite page: reprint of a newspa[per]
article that first appeared on Apri[l]
1941. The Andrews Journal reprinted
1941 article on September 13, 19[__]
(collection of Jim King)*

RHODO, APRIL 7, 1941.. A disastrous train wreck at 2:20 p.m. here today, killed both engineer Fred Thompson Bourne, 52 of Asheville and fireman John Q. Zimmerman, 48, also of Asheville, both being instantly killed when Passenger Train No. 17 out of Asheville bound for Murphy, on the Western Carolina Division of the Richmond & Danville Railroad of the Southern Railway System, jumped the tracks and overturned in Valley River, alongside the Railroad grade and between the Railway and Highway No. 19, in process of being relocated. The Engineer died of a broken neck, and the Fireman of a fractured skull. The Engineer died of a broken neck, both men being pronounced dead at the sceneby Dr. Harry Miller, M.D. of Murphy. A team of investigators for the Interstate Commerce Commission is reported to have concluded that the engineer had "kicked off the brakes and was working steam" down the mountain in an effort to make up lost time and that the heavy Pacific Type Locomotive No. 1278, was going at a speed in excess of fifty miles per hour when it left the rails. The regular engineer for the run, G. C. (Stonewall) Jackson had turned the engine over to Bourne at Nantahala, and takinghis lunch box with him, had gone back to sit with the Conductor in the single passenger car, in the rear. Bourne had been a former engineer but had been demoted back to fireman during the depression, because of reduction in car loadings and lack of work. He had just a short time before, been promoted back to engineer and was making a number of trail runs over different divisions, before returning to full time duty, as engineer. The railway Post Office, express and baggage car which was also one-half smoking car, in the immediate rear of the engine, broke loose and swung around, sliding down the bank or fill of the railroad grade, without overturning, while the passenger car, coupled to it, broke loose, and with the front trucks or journal, derailed and riding the ties, went on down the track for some distance, when it struck a big rock and stopped, with the rear wheels or journal, still on the rails and the car, remaining upright. Apparently there were no other injuries to crew or passengers. Several crates of Indian Game Chickens, being shipped to Murphy, were in the express and baggage car, and remained intact and were delivered later by truck. The pile of express packages and mail, stacked on the railroad track, to theleft of the mail and express car, contained a crate of oranges and grapefruit consigned to Tom Hay of Aquone Road, Valleytown, by his father, Neil Hay, then in Florida. Tom Hay working for Utah Constructon Company, contractors for Nantahala Power Company, then building Nantahala Dam at Aquone, just happened to be passing in a truck at thetime and Tom Hay, with the help of the late Vic Matoy and the Master Mechnaic for Gregory and Pool, contractors on the rebuilding and relocation of present Highway No. 19 (whose name nobody now seems to remember) working as volunteers and at considerable pesonal risk , removed the bodies of both Engineer Bourne and Fireman Zimmerman, from beneath the upsidedown locomotive, the bodies being taken back to Asheville for funeral and burial there. Tom Hay said it was necessary to use a cutting torch - borrowed from theHighway contractors at the scene - to free the Fireman and Vic Matoy provided a saw to cut timber and brush holding Bourne's body. Tom Hay recalled that Bourne's fine Railroad Gold Watch was still running, when his body was removed from the wreckage but that a thief in the large crowd present, stole the watch before the body of Bourne could be covered by some canvas or sheets provided - he thinks, by the family of Lyle Bryson, who lived near the scene. The wreck occurred between the railroad crossing at Lyle Bryson's and the trestle near where Tommy Higdon now lives--on a sharp curve and high fill and quite a steep grade, on the roadroad. Stonewall Jackson, the regular engineer, lunch pail in hand, dismounted from the passener car, cameback up the railroad track, walked across the upside down engine No. 1278 and peering down, at the partly exposed bodies of Bourne and Zimmerman, is reported to have said: "There, but for the Grace of God - I might be!" He climbed to the grade of Highway 19 and flagging a passing car, caught a ride back to Asheville and did not return to service as an Engineer on the Murphy Branch. Locomotive No. 1278, was not a total loss, however, it being pulled back to the tracks by heavy duty cranes and after being dead-headed back to Asheville, was transhipped to Coster Railroad Shops of the Southern at Knoxville where it was rebuilt and-returned to service, Tom Hay later saw it pulling local freight at Lenoir City, Tennessee, between Knoxville and Chattanooga, originally known as East Tennessee-Virginia Railroad.

(93.1) *See story on page 115.*   *(Andrews Journal 9-13-72, collection of Jim King)*

Smoky Mountains Railroad is crossed. It is eleven feet long. The grade has reduced to 2.5%. Mile **93.9** also marks the community of Rhodo.

94 Will Sandlin Tunnel

At mile **94.2**, there was a 171-foot-long siding on the left called Davis Siding. The train will pass through a very scenic area with the grade becoming steeper - 3.4%. A 13 degree left turn is at mile **94.7**. At mile **94.8**, the Valley River is again crossed on a right curving 106-foot-long trestle. Immediately after crossing the bridge, you will enter the 335-foot-long Will Sandlin Tunnel. The track through the tunnel is straight, but the grade is still descending at 2.9%. Exiting the tunnel, you will again cross the Valley River on another trestle, 104 feet long.

95 Valley River Crossings

This mile begins with a 13 degree left curve. After the curve, there is a short straight followed by a 9 degree right curve. In this curve, there are two

117

crossings of the Valley River on trestles, each over 100 feet long. Tom Thumb Creek flows into the Valley River, now on the right side of the train.

96 Tallest Trestle

At mile **96.2**, the grade reduces to 0.2% for about a quarter of a mile. At mile **96.6**, there is a wood trestle in an 8-degree curve to the right. This is the tallest wood trestle on Great Smoky Mountains Railroad at 31 feet high. It is 136 feet long. Of course, it is the Valley River that is crossed.

(Michael George photos)

118

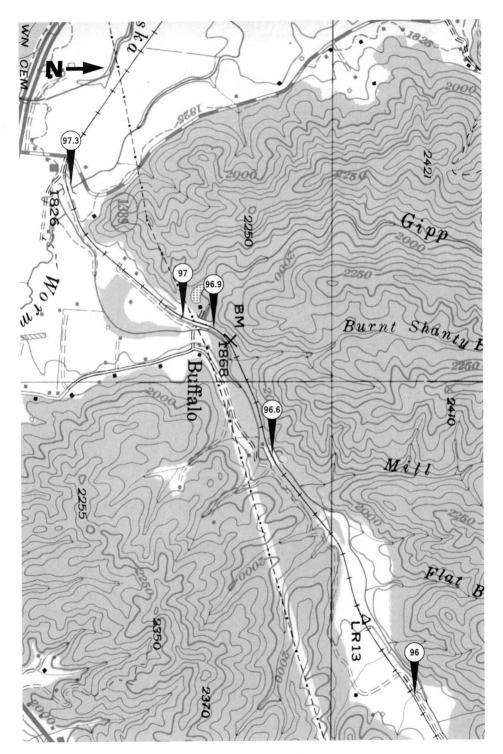

After this point, the grade increases to 1.6%. Supposedly, three wild goats live in this area and are occasionally seen near the track.

97 Death Valley

The train is about to leave the confined mountainous area and enter a valley. At mile **97.3**, the last crossing of the Valley River is made. The bridge for once is not a wood trestle but a steel through plate girder 81 feet long. The last steel bridge was at Fontana Lake. The train now enters Death Valley, so named because of the large amount of vultures that perch on the fences

Through plate girder bridge at mile 97.3.   *(Michael George photos)*

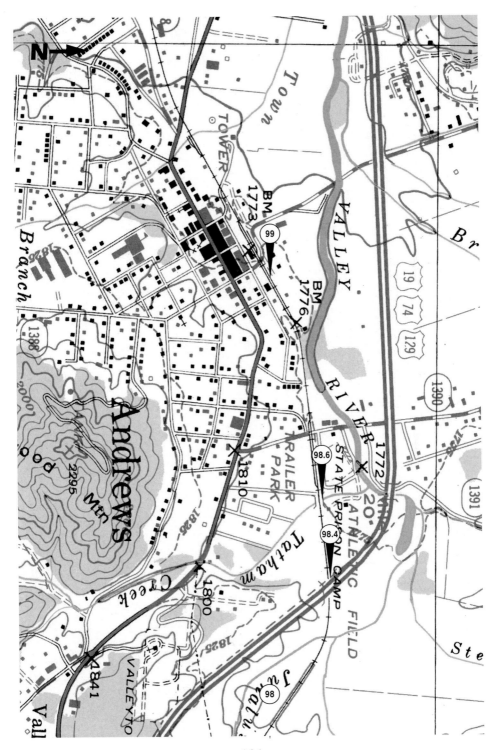

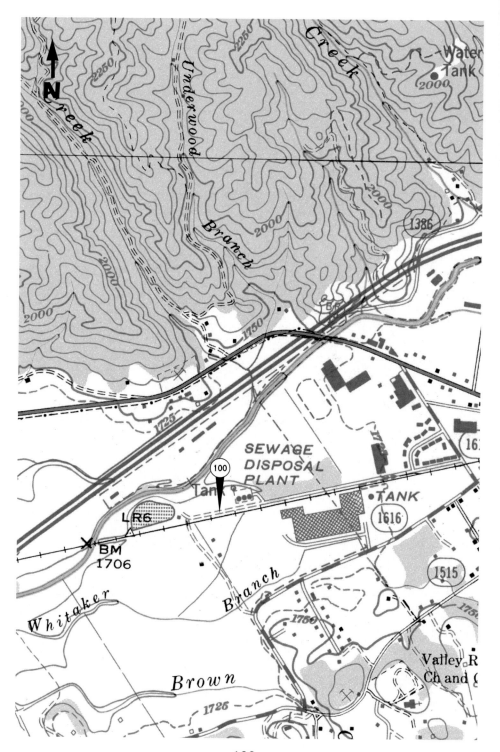

The depot at Andrews, 1967. Note semaphore on roof. Great Smoky Mountains Railroad has built a new depot here.

along the track. It gets very hot in this valley in the summer, with no trees for shade, and track maintenance workers think the vultures are waiting for them to die from heat exhaustion. Cattle frequently get on the track here also. This section of track has had many ties replaced recently. The grade is now only 0.7%.

98 Andrews

At mile **98.3** the train will cross Junaluska Creek on a wood trestle. The Highway 74 overpass is at mile **98.4**. Another trestle is crossed at mile **98.6**. This 130 foot long trestle was extensively rebuilt by Great Smoky Mountains Railroad in the summer of 2000. Immediately after the trestle, on the left, was the interchange with the Ritter Lumber Company. There were several tracks. This railroad went for many miles to the southeast, reaching elevations of over 3000 feet. Through a series of switchbacks, it eventually reached the Nantahala River, following it for several miles. It had to be abandoned in the early forties when Nantahala Dam was constructed. The Parker-Reichman grain elevators occupy the location of the interchange with the Southern Railway in Andrews. Parker Reichman is Great Smoky Mountains Railroad's biggest freight customer.

99 Andrews Depot

The Andrews depot is at Milepost 99. This is not the original depot. Great Smoky Mountains Railway built the depot in 1990. Several bed and breakfasts are in Andrews. The rail trip ends here, but Great Smoky Mountains Railroad owns track to Milepost 100. At mile **99.5**, a large tannery, the Cherokee Extract Tanning Co., operated on the south side of the track at one time. At Milepost 100, the Tennessee and North Carolina Railroad interchanged with the Southern. This logging line eventually went to the Hiwassee River, following it to Hayesville, North Carolina.

(99) *Andrews Depot on a foggy morning, September 2000.*   *(Frank Strack photo)*

Chapter 3

Bryson City to Wesser- Before 1944

The route of the Murphy Branch prior to 1945 was much different than it is today. For one, it was about eight and a half miles longer. Rather than cross the Tuckasegee at Bryson City, it followed the north bank of the river downstream to Bushnell, a small community at the point where the Tuckasegee flows into the Little Tennessee river. At Bushnell, there was a junction with the trackage of the Carolina and Tennessee Southern Railway Company. The Carolina and Tennessee Southern, owned by the Southern, followed the Little Tennessee downstream for 13.96 miles to Fontana. The Southern crossed the Tuckasegee and followed the Little Tennessee upstream for about three miles. At Indian Ridge, the river made a horseshoe turn with some sharp bends. The railroad tunneled through Indian Ridge instead and crossed the river. At Almond, the Nantahala river flows into the Little Tennessee. The railroad crossed the Nantahala, followed it upstream for about three miles, then crossed it again. There were two more crossings at Wesser Creek. This route may have been longer, but the grades were relatively easy because of following the river valleys.

There were many small communities in this area, and many people lived in them. Leaving Bryson City, the first was Epp's Springs, then Noland, at milepost T 71, which had a station. There was a school at Epp's Springs. Forney was next, but there was no station there, just a siding. Bushnell, milepost T 77, had a station along with a hotel across the tracks from it. There was also a school, a church, and a general store. There was a water tank at milepost T 77.7, which was between Bushnell and Judson. Judson had a couple of sidings. Almond, milepost T 85, had a station, a high school, and at least one church.

Bushnell was the beginning of the Carolina and Tennessee Southern. There was a small yard at Bushnell with seventy-five car capacity. There were three communities served by C&TS, Marcus, milepost TA 9, Ritter, milepost TA 12, and Fontana at milepost 13.9. At milepost TA 7, there was the Wayside water tank. At Fontana, a narrow gauge railroad connected

The Bushnell depot in April 1943. The general store is across the tracks in the background. (TVA photo, courtesy of Federal Records Center)

The general store and hotel across from the depot in Bushnell in April, 1943. Bryson City is to the right, Fontana by way of the Carolina and Tennessee Southern is to the left. (TVA photo, courtesy of Federal Records Center)

126

The Indian Ridge Tunnel in April 1943, looking west toward Murphy. It is under Fontana lake now, but when the water level is right, it is possible to take a boat through it.

(TVA photo, courtesy of Federal Records Center)

This is Nantahala #2 at milepost T87, about a mile east of Wesser Creek. Construction is in progress on the new relocated line in the background, April 28, 1943.

(TVA photo, courtesy of Federal Records Center)

with the C&TS. It served the Fontana Copper Mine that was located about three miles up Eagle creek. There was another copper mine near Proctor on Hazel Creek called the Adams mine.[33]

Copper ore was shipped in wooden-sided composite hoppers. Three or four cars would be set out in Bushnell for the Bryson City to Murphy train to pick up. They would take them to Andrews and weigh them on the scale. Then, they were transported to Murphy and interchanged with the L&N to go on to Copper Hill. A lot of wood was also loaded. In the early forties every trip to Fontana would yield at least three carloads of copper ore.

The area supported lots of farming, although one would not think so from the way it looks today. However, what is now lake bottom used to be fertile river valleys. Due to the abundance of timber, many people made a living cutting wood and transporting it to the nearest siding, where it could be loaded on to rack cars and taken to the paper mills.

At Bushnell, the Southern crossed the Tuckasegee on a wood pile trestle. At the Indian Ridge tunnel, it crossed the Little Tennessee River on the south side of the tunnel. This crossing was also on a wood pile trestle. The tunnel was about six hundred feet long and was bored through solid rock. The Nantahala crossing at Almond, called Nantahala No. 1, was made on seven deck plate girder bridges with a wood pile trestle approach on the north end. This crossing is visible today from Great Smoky Mountains Railroad when the water in Fontana Lake is low enough. There are still some ties visible in the roadbed.

The next crossing was at milepost T 87, Nantahala No. 2. It was a one hundred sixty-nine-foot pin-connected through truss bridge built in 1898 by the Phoenix Bridge Company. The western approach to the bridge was on a wood pile trestle. The east abutment and concrete pier are visible at low water from the Great Smoky Mountains Railroad.

At Wesser Creek, there were two more crossings of the Nantahala. There was a horseshoe shaped bend in the river and rather than have the sharp curves, the railroad used six hundred feet of deck plate girder bridges to make the crossings.[34] There was a small siding at Wesser Creek, and wood was loaded there. There was also a general store. The railroad frequently unloaded roofing materials and feed there.

U.S. Highway number 19 used to come through Almond. It roughly paralleled Siles Branch into Almond. It crossed the Little Tennessee River on a concrete bridge and began climbing a ridge on the east side of the river.

The road is still visible at low water. The earth has washed out from under the pavement due to wave action, but slabs of concrete are visible where they have slid down the bank. It is also possible to see the bridge site, and the roadbed leading to it on each side.

The railroad between Almond and Bushnell, plus the Carolina and Tennessee Southern, almost became part of a much larger system. The Tallulah Falls Railway was another Southern owned shortline. The southern end had a junction with the Southern's Washington to Atlanta mainline at Cornelia, Georgia. The northern end terminated in Franklin, North Carolina. The last nineteen miles of the line followed the Little Tennessee River from Rabun Gap to Franklin.[35]

In the early 1900's, the Southern Railway was planning many construction projects. The Southern had a desire to connect Knoxville with the Washington-Atlanta mainline near the Georgia-South Carolina border. This route would pass through the Great Smoky and Blue Ridge mountains. From Knoxville, sixteen miles were already in place with the Knoxville & Augusta Railroad that ran to Maryville, Tennessee. Another line was built around 1905 from Maryville to Calderwood on the Little Tennessee River. This line was thirty-one miles long and was called the Tennessee & Carolina Southern. Then, there was the Bushnell to Fontana Carolina and Tennessee Southern. In a straight line, Calderwood and Fontana were only twelve miles apart. So, there were only two gaps to fill in, between Almond and Franklin and Fontana and Calderwood, and the route would have been complete. It also would have been a water-level route.[36]

This very scenic line was never completed, though. There was a financial panic in 1907 that probably put a stop to this project along with several others. It was felt that the current Knoxville to Atlanta line through Cleveland, Tennessee and the other to Spartanburg, South Carolina, by way of Saluda, were adequate without adding a third line. Also, the two remaining stretches to be constructed would pass through some very rugged terrain. Extensive excavation and tunneling would have been required.[37] If it had been completed, the relocation project required by the construction of Fontana dam would have been nearly impossible due to the mountainous terrain.

The old community of Almond is in the valley, the new one is behind the train. A Ks class consolidation is pulling a work train in 1944.
    (Frank Clodfelter photo, courtesy of Great Smoky Mountains Railroad)

Old Nantahala River crossing in 1985 taken from the new relocated track. The Little Tennessee River is in the background. The old Hwy. 19 crossing is barely visible on the Little Tennessee River. (Michael George photo)

Chapter 4
The Fontana Relocation

The United States entry into W.W.II created tremendous demands on every type of industry. More electrical power was needed for the businesses producing war material. The Tennessee Valley Authority's Fontana Dam was constructed during the war as part of the emergency program. It would have been a huge project during peacetime considering the problems of design, access, housing, manpower, and materials in a remote wilderness area. Due to the war, the project was scheduled for completion in half the time it would normally take. The construction of Fontana Dam received attention of civil engineers world wide. It is the highest dam in the Eastern United States at 480 feet and when it was completed in 1944 it was the fourth largest dam in the world.

Construction of the reservoir would flood twenty-four miles of the Murphy Branch between Bryson City and Wesser because the railroad followed three different rivers that would become lake bottom. Only two years were allocated for relocating the railroad, and this included surveys, design, and construction. Since steel was a critical material, no new steel could be used in the relocation. In light of the rugged terrain in this area, it seemed an almost impossible task for the engineers to design a new right of way with no bridges. To avoid use of steel, heavy grading was required, causing some fills to exceed one hundred feet in height. In some places, though, bridges could not be eliminated. When the use of a bridge could not be avoided, spans from other relocations or from the old right of way were used.[38] This was the last major railroad construction in the United States until the Powder River coal fields were developed in Wyoming during the 1980's.

When the final route was decided, it was 15.98 miles long, 8.4 miles shorter than the old line through Bushnell.[39]

The contract between the Southern and TVA specified that TVA would be responsible for constructing a new main track between milepost T64 in Bryson City and T88.5 in Wesser with a 0.9% compensated maximum grade for eastbound traffic and a 1.3% compensated maximum grade for west-bound traffic. Compensated grade takes into account both the actual grade incline and the effect of friction in curves. TVA was to prepare the grade, roadbed, and track, including bridges, culverts, and embankments. When finished, trains would be able to run over the new line just as they had on the old one. TVA would also build a new wye in Bryson City for turning locomotives. The new right of way was planned to extend one hundred feet on either side of the center line of the track. TVA would remove the 169 foot pin connected truss at milepost T87, remodel it into a riveted type, and install it over the Tuckasegee River in Bryson City. Four steel truss bridges removed from another relocation project on the French Broad River near Leadvale, Tennessee, were scheduled to be used for crossing the Little Tennessee River near Almond. At Wesser Creek the channel of the Nantahala River was to be altered so two bridges could be removed and used elsewhere. TVA was also responsible for removing all salvageable ties, bridges, and other usable track material from the old line and loading it on rail cars. TVA additionally guaranteed that the existing Murphy Branch would be continuously available for operation.[40]

The Southern Railway was responsible for providing work train service, removing and relaying track, and moving and installing telegraph, telephone, and signal lines. TVA agreed to cover the expenses involved for this work. The Railroad also had to agree to transfer deed of the abandoned right of way to the United States of America.[41]

The new route, being 8.4 miles shorter, follows a more direct route between Bryson City and Wesser Creek. The new route was to roughly parallel the existing roadbed in the Nantahala River gorge from Wesser to Almond, where the Nantahala flows into the Little Tennessee River. This is a distance of about five miles. Unfortunately for the grading crews, this involved cutting a shelf into the side of the almost precipitous Nantahala Gorge. The new roadbed alignment leaves Wesser and is generally level, leaving the old line which was only a few feet above the river. In many places along this stretch of track the new grade was directly above the old one. Timbers were placed perpendicular to the ties between the rails and outside the rails. It looked almost like a continuous grade crossing. These timbers protected the track from slides during the grading and blasting above. If material did get on the track, it could be easily removed with bulldozers. One such slide blocked traffic for several hours on March 8, 1943. At Al-

This photo was taken on March 8, 1943. A slide has occurred across the track a little east of Wesser. Passenger train 18 has been stopped by the slide. Number 68, the doubleheaded eastbound freight, has been stopped also. TVA construction equipment is frantically trying to clear the track since TVA guaranteed no interruptions to traffic.

(TVA photo, courtesy of Federal Records Center)

mond, the new line ceases to follow the main river valleys and follows Alarka Creek valley through a gap in Jackson Line Mountain. Between this gap and the Tuckasegee River crossing in Bryson City, it follows Buckner Branch valley.[42]

Bryson City is at elevation 1730 feet. The highest pool level for Fontana Dam is 1717 feet. Wesser is at elevation 1722 feet. Bushnell was at elevation 1474 feet. Thus, when the lake is at its fullest level, Bushnell is 243 feet below the surface.

As mentioned earlier, the truss bridge at the Tuckasegee River in Bryson City came from the Nantahala no. 2. crossing. To maintain Murphy Branch traffic, a temporary crossing had to be made at Nantahala number two. This crossing was located on the downstream side of the truss bridge quite close to the truss. At low water level, the abutments for the truss bridge and the roadbed leading to the temporary crossing are easily seen. After being disassembled, the bridge was then loaded on rail cars and shipped to Bryson City for reconstruction at the Tuckasegee crossing. The four 63-foot-long deck girder bridges used with the truss bridge at Bryson City came from the Cherokee Dam construction site near Morristown, Tennessee. They were manu-

The relocated Nantahala #2 truss bridge is now over the Tuckasegee River in Bryson City. A dumptruck can be seen under the first deck girder bridge under the hopper car. Material could be dumped from cars on the bridge into a truck through this temporary set-up. The view is looking east toward Bryson City. The date is April 28, 1944.

(TVA photo, courtesy of Federal Records Center)

factured in 1940 by the Mount Vernon Bridge Company and modified for the Tuckasegee crossing. This made the overall length of the bridge 426 feet. The Tuckasegee River crossing was completed by April, 1944. The first girder bridge was temporarily modified so hopper cars could dump materials into dump trucks underneath.

The approach to the Tuckasegee bridge from the Bryson City side passed directly through the location of the turning wye. The wye was moved to a location just west of the depot. The engineers' goal was to make the Tuckasegee crossing use the least amount of bridge steel. To accomplish this, the approach on the other end would interfere with U.S. Highway 19. Since concrete was more readily available than steel, .52 mile of Highway 19 was relocated and paved with concrete.[43] Original plans called for the crossing to be made much closer to Bryson City. The crossing would be made a little west of the depot, where the wye was moved. The river widens here and there is an island. However, this alignment would require two grade crossings of Highway 19. Grade crossings of major highways are avoided as much as possible due to safety and traffic flow concerns.

An underpass was required at milepost T71.6 where the track crosses old North Carolina State Highway 10. This was built using a creosote timber trestle 77 feet long. This trestle is located in a ten and a half degree curve, one of the sharpest on the relocation.

A concrete arch bridge is used for the crossing of Alarka Creek at about milepost T73. The roadbed is on a fill which is 75 feet high. The concrete bridge is 172 feet long with the actual arch 26 feet high. Other concrete structures included four arch culverts from 10 by 10 feet to 16 by 16 feet. Seven box culverts were used ranging from 5 by 8 feet to 8 by 12 feet. A total of 8,800 linear feet of concrete pipe culverts were used, varying from 24 to 72 inches in diameter.[44]

The most extensive bridge work was required at the Little Tennessee River crossing, which is about a mile east of Almond. This bridge is 777 feet long, consisting of four 157-foot through truss spans and two 67-foot deck plate girder spans. The reinforced concrete piers that support the trusses are 160 feet high. This was quite a civil engineering feat. The five concrete piers were constructed first. A temporary bridge for vehicle crossing was built at the base of the piers. The first plate girder bridge was then set in place by a crane on the western abutment and the first pier. Since the treads on the crane were wider than the girder bridge, large beams were then laid across the bridge, twice the length of the crawler crane. The crane moved onto the bridge. When it reached the end of the beams, the ones not under the crane were picked up and moved in front of it. In this fashion, the crane could move forward to the end of the first girder and set the second one in place. Then, it could move to the end of the second one in the same manner.

The truss bridges presented more of a challenge. The concrete piers and two girder bridges were finished by November of 1943. The trusses had been disassembled for transportation to the site. A large platform almost the length of the truss was made up from four plate girders assembled side by side. This was carefully lifted into place by the crane. Temporary piers made from wood and steel were used to support this platform. This gave a surface for placing the many small deck plate girders that make up the track support for a truss bridge. Once they were in place, the crane could move onto them and assemble the truss. Each of the four trusses was assembled in this manner, working toward the east end of the bridge. Trains were travelling across the bridge by July of 1944.

The crane is visible lifting the platform in place for erecting the truss bridges. The old line is clearly visible. November 23, 1944. (TVA photo, courtesy of Federal Records Center)

The piers to the Little Tennessee River crossing November 23, 1943. The old line is visible along the river. The platform used for erecting the truss bridges is being lifted into place by the crane at the west end of the bridge. (TVA photo, courtesy of Federal Records Center)

Three of the Little Tennessee River truss bridges are in place. The fourth one's deck girders are on top of timbers placed on the temporary platform. Truss erection will follow. Notice the 172-foot-high temporary pier holding the platform. April 28, 1944.

(TVA photo, courtesy of Federal Records Center)

Ks-1 #712 is leading a train across the completed Little Tennessee River bridge on July 26, 1944. *(TVA photo, courtesy of Federal Records Center)*

The date is January 23, 1943, at Wesser. One of the old line's deck girder bridges is visible. The Nantahala River channel has not yet been relocated. Taken from Highway 19, looking east. *(TVA photo, courtesy of Federal Records Center)*

One more temporary crossing for the railroad was required in addition to the temporary crossing at Nantahala # 2. This one was between Almond and the Little Tennessee River crossing. The old line crossed the Nantahala River where Turkey Creek flowed into the river. This portion of the line for about a mile on the west side of the Nantahala River was directly in the path of the new line. A temporary pile trestle was built across the Nantahala where it flows into the Little Tennessee. Track was laid from Almond to this new crossing, freeing the west side of the river for the huge fill that was constructed across Turkey Creek. The entire valley across the mouth of Turkey Creek was filled. This fill explains why the bridge piers visible at low water appear to go directly into the side of the mountain. That mountain was not there before 1944. The total amount of excavated material for the entire 15.98 mile relocation was 3,790,000 cubic yards, with much of it being stone.[45] When water is low enough in the lake, it is possible to park at the Almond Boat Dock and walk down to the old roadbed. The roadbed can be walked all the way to the concrete piers for the Nantahala River crossing. There are still some ties in place, and tie plates and spikes, along with ballast, are visible, even though they have been submerged for more than fifty years. Walking north to where the Nantahala flows into the Little Tennessee, the remnants of the temporary pile trestle are visible, as well as

The date is February 24, 1945. The view is looking west at Wesser. The Nantahala River's new channel is on the left. The old channel curved to the right behind the cut. Previously, there were two railroad bridges here. Highway 19 is on the left, where it leaves the Nantahala Gorge. A bridge is visible in the background over the river. This bridge serves Nantahala Outdoor Center today.   *(TVA photo, courtesy of Federal Records Center)*

The temporary crossing of the Nantahala on the old line used when the Turkey Creek fill was made.   *(Michael George photo)*

This photo is taken from the current location of Almond Boat Dock. The Little Tennessee River crossing is in the background. The relocated old line to avoid the Turkey Creek fill is visible in the center of the picture. Highway 19 crosses the river and climbs the ridge. The date is May 24, 1944. The concrete slabs of the highway are visible today at low water levels. *(TVA photo, courtesy of Federal Records Center)*

The old line crossed the Nantahala River at Almond. Ties still lie on the roadbed after being submerged more than 50 years. *(Michael George photo)*

140

Train 17 is about to get deep into the Nantahala Gorge at Wesser, May 23, 1947. The old roadbed from Wesser to Almond is visible in the foreground. The first deck girder bridge on the old line was below the rear passenger car. Taken from Highway 19.

(R.D. Sharpless photo, Frank Ardrey collection)

the temporary roadbed leading to it. Remnants of the Highway 19 crossing of the Little Tennessee are also visible.

The sharpest curve on the relocation occurs where there is a 125-degree bend in the Nantahala River. This point is about halfway between Wesser and Almond. The old line was on the east side of the river, so it could follow a gentler curvature. The new line, on the west side, is in the precipitous rock wall of the canyon. This curve is 14 degrees. There are two 12-degree curves and six 10-degree curves on the relocation. The rest of the curves are 8 degrees or less. The total curvature for the relocation in degrees is 2,341 which is an average of 153 degrees per mile. This was not considered excessive when compared to the old line or other railroads traversing similar mountainous topography.[46]

Some of the fills presented engineering problems since they would be submerged to depths greater than 100 feet. The deepest cut on the relocation is 153 feet and the highest fill is 130 feet. This lake was designed to fluctuate as much as 185 feet so this created concerns about wave action on

This photo, taken from the new highway bridge at Almond, shows the old line and the old Almond depot. The Little Tennessee River bridge is in the background. A train is visible in the background also. A fill has covered the road at the end of the old highway bridge in Almond. The date is August 23, 1944.   (TVA photo, courtesy of Federal Records Center)

The new Almond depot. GP38 #2859 is eastbound with train 72 in July 1988.

(Jim King photo)

The Alarka Creek Valley looking west. Note the many deep cuts and high fills plus the farmland that is now lake bottom. The date is November 23, 1943.

(TVA photo, courtesy of Federal Records Center)

This picture was taken on July 26, 1944, four days before the new line officially opened. The lead locomotive is number 712, Ks-1. There are thirty-nine cars in the train. It is headed east, about to cross the Tuckasegee River into Bryson City. A brakeman is standing on top of a boxcar about halfway back into the train. (TVA photo, courtesy of Federal Records Center)

the fills. In these places, the outer two feet of the embankment was to be composed of 70 percent stone one cubic foot or larger. [47]

The channel of the Nantahala River was altered at Wesser Creek. Previously the river made a horseshoe bend around a small ridge. There were two bridges on the old line made from 600 feet of deck plate girders. The channel was changed so it flowed straight, paralleling the railroad. This eliminated the bridges and freed more steel for use elsewhere. The excavation at Wesser entailed 60,000 cubic yards of material, most of which was solid rock.[48] This also created quite a set of rapids which are now popular with white water enthusiasts. A short walk on the west side of the track reveals the old channel which still has water in it. The old line's roadbed also begins here and can be walked, when water in the lake is low enough, to the location of the Nantahala # 2 crossing.

Heaviest traffic on the Murphy Branch was eastbound. With this in mind, the engineers designed the ruling grade in that direction to be 0.90 percent. Between the Little Tennessee River crossing and the summit at Jackson Line Gap, the line climbs for about five miles at 0.90 percent. Descending from the gap towards Bryson City the maximum grade is 1.3 percent. This grade is separated into two portions with a 0.7 mile stretch of 0.43 percent grade.[49] There is a horseshoe curve in this portion.

Two sidings were added on the relocated line. McLain was about half a mile east of the Little Tennessee River bridge in a long straight section of track. Brooks siding was just west of the crest at Jackson Line Gap where Highway 19 parallels the track. Both were double ended, but McLain was much longer. The westbound Blue Goose would often meet the eastbound Blue Goose here. When traffic on the Branch slowed down in the 1960's, the sidings were removed. There is a bluff between McLain siding and the bridge on the right side of the track going west. For several years, railroaders on the trains saw wild goats there.

The entire community of Almond at milepost T85.3 was submerged by the lake. The new community of Almond is at milepost T77. A highway bridge was built here that is 727 feet long. It crosses the Nantahala River and the Murphy Branch. It rests on concrete piers 125 feet high. A siding was also built.

The Carolina and Tennessee Southern (the line between Bushnell and Fontana) played an important role in the construction of Fontana Dam. The community of Fontana was about a mile and a half upstream from the dam construction site. The railroad would have to be extended so materials could be transported to the dam. A timber trestle was built over Eagle Creek and tracks were extended 2.84 miles along the bank of the Little Tennessee River. A yard, located north of the dam site, was built with four tracks that could hold one hundred cars each. There was a runaround track so locomotives headed west could escape from their train and return to the east end so they could switch. This was the destination for the fifty-car trains of cement from Bryson City. This yard became an extremely busy place for the duration of the construction. At the dam site, a 1127-foot-long tunnel was bored under the west side of the dam so the tracks could continue to the shop area. There were sidings for the machine shop, warehouse, carpenter shop, and storage areas. TVA used small mining-type locomotives to switch cars from the tunnel to their shops. Southern Railway locomotives were not allowed in the tunnel. Southern Railway placed the loaded cement cars on the tracks at the unloader, but TVA was responsible for removing empty cars and shoving full ones to the unloader. The boxcars of cement had wood in the doorways to keep the cement from spilling. The cement was loaded in bulk, blown into the ends of the cars first to distribute the weight over the trucks.

Plans called for 2,800,000 cubic yards of concrete in the dam construction. The construction schedule required 200,000 yards per month, which is 8,000 cubic yards a day. To support the concrete use, 15,000 tons of gravel and sand a day would be required. This equals 300 two-bay hopper cars delivered every day. Since this placed incredible traffic demands on the railroad, and there wasn't enough yard storage room available at the dam site, the decision was made to build a quarry about a mile downstream of the dam.[50]

The cement unloading area was located upstream from the dam so the rail tunnel wouldn't be clogged with excess traffic. Reinforcing steel and other materials were unloaded in the shop areas. Two tracks went to the cement unloader which was under a steel shed. The boxcars of cement came from Signal Mountain in Chattanooga, Volunteer in Knoxville, and two Penn-Dixie plants in Richard City and Kingsport.

The cement trains were run in the morning as extras from Bryson City. They were powered by one Ks class Consolidation running tender first. There was no wye for turning locomotives on the Carolina and Tennessee Southern. The one locomotive could easily handle the train since it was downhill all the way from Bryson City to Fontana. The cement trains came into Bryson

City in the evening, pulled by double-headed 2-8-0's, and returned to Asheville with empty boxcars. Other supplies such as wood and steel were shipped over the railroad also. For a mile or so on the mainline, trucks backed up to the freight cars so materials could be loaded onto the trucks.

The Southern Railway filed for abandonment of the Murphy Branch between milepost T64.5 and T88.2 on September 25, 1943 as required by contract with TVA. The Interstate Commerce Commission approved it and the new line opened for use on July 30, 1944. The Carolina and Tennessee Southern Railway filed for abandonment on July 31, 1943. The property owned by the railroad was deeded to the United States of America on May 12, 1944 and the track materials were sold to the Southern Railway on June 29, 1944. The line had been completely dismantled by December 1, 1944.[51]

Fontana switcher crew in 1943. Left to right is Tom Sandlin, Conductor; L.A. Wright, Flagman; Grady Hyde, fireman; Joe Sawyer, engineer; and Lake Simpson, brakeman. Ks-2 engine 711 is behind them. *(Photo from J. T. Earwood collection)*

Chapter 5
Great Smoky Mountains Railroad Equipment

Steam locomotive No. 1702 at GSMRR's shop, July 2000.   *(Frank Strack photo)*

Locomotives
Steam Locomotive No. 1702

Probably the most famous piece of equipment on Great Smoky Mountains Railroad is locomotive 1702. This 2-8-0 Consolidation was originally built by Baldwin for the U.S. Army in 1942. The engine was built to operate on European railroads which have tighter tolerances on tunnels and bridges. Therefore, the cab, stack, and sandbox were smaller than they would be on their American counterpart. The 1702 never went overseas, though.

In 1947 the Army sold it to the Warren & Saline River Railroad in Arkansas. In 1964 it was sold to the Reader Railroad in Arkansas, a tourist line. While the 1702 was at Reader, it was converted from a coal burner to an oil burner. In 1982, it was sold to the Freemont and Elkhorn Northern in Nebraska. It remained there until it was purchased by Great Smoky Mountains Railway in 1991.

Great Smoky Mountains Railroad has altered the appearance of 1702 to make it look more like an American steam locomotive: the stack has been raised, the sandbox modified, and the cab widened. Greg Dodd, engine master at the GSMRR shop, has made mechanical improvements also. The friction bearings on the four driving axles have been replaced with roller bearings, greatly increasing the life of the bearings and reducing friction. No. 1702 was used in the movie "This Property is Condemned," starring Natalie Wood, Charles Bronson, and Robert Redford.

Diesel Locomotive No. 711 at Bryson City Depot July 2000.   (*Frank Strack photo*)

Diesel Locomotive No. 711

Number 711 was a 1500 horsepower EMD GP-7 when built in 1953. When built, it was used on the Chicago and Northwestern Railway as No. 4400. It was used in the movie "Forces of Nature," starring Sandra Bullock and Ben Afleck. The cab end of the locomotive has been modified to a "low short hood" to increase visibility for the crew. The locomotive has been upgraded to GP-9 specifications which increases the horsepower to 1750.

Diesel Locomotive No. 777 at the GSMRR's shop, July 2000.   *(Frank Strack photo)*

Diesel Locomotive No. 777

Number 777 is also a 1500 horsepower EMD GP-7 built in 1953 for the Chicago and Northwestern as No. 4282. It was used as the power engine in the movie "The Fugitive," starring Harrison Ford and Tommy Lee Jones. The cab end of the locomotive has been modified to a "low short hood" or "chopped nose" to increase visibility for the crew.

Diesel Locomotive No. 210

Diesel Locomotive No. 210 being worked on at GSMRR's shop, July 2000. (Frank Strack photo)

Number 210 is a 2500 horsepower EMD GP-35 built in 1964 and originally used on the Norfolk and Western as No. 210. The cab end of the locomotive has been modified to a "low short hood" to increase visibility for the crew. It was used in the movies "My Fellow Americans" and "Forces of Nature."

Diesel Locomotive No. 223

Number 223 is a 2500 horsepower EMD GP-35 built in 1964 and originally used on the Norfolk and Western as No. 223. The cab end of the locomotive has been modified to a "low short hood" to increase visibility for the crew. It was used in the movies "My Fellow Americans" and "Forces of Nature."

Diesel Locomotive No. 223 at the Bryson City Depot July 2000.   *(Frank Strack photo)*

Passenger Cars

Car 25 Piedmont

Built in 1926, the car is a heavyweight coach with three axle trucks. It was built for the Southern Railway and was later office car #25 on Conrail. It was rebuilt in 1991 by Great Smoky Mountains Railway.

Car 26 Southland

Built in 1926, the car is a heavyweight coach with three axle trucks. It

150

also came from the Southern Railway and was later used as office car #26 on Conrail. It was rebuilt in 1988 by Great Smoky Mountains Railway.

Car 320 Sylva

Built in 1921, the car is a heavyweight coach with three axle trucks. It is thought that this car was originally owned by the Louisville and Nashville. It was rebuilt by Great Smoky Mountains Railway in 1989.

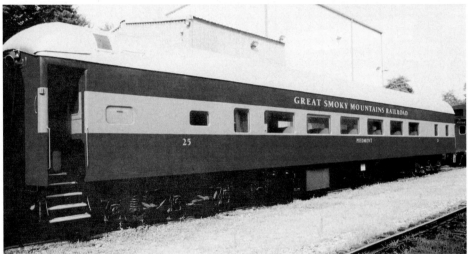

Car 25 Piedmont.   *(Michael George photo)*

Car 26 Southland.   *(Frank Strack photo)*

Car 322 Bryson City

This car is also believed to have come from the L&N. It is a heavy-weight coach with three axle trucks. The car was built in 1921 and rebuilt in 1989.

Car 322 Bryson City.   *(Frank Strack photo)*

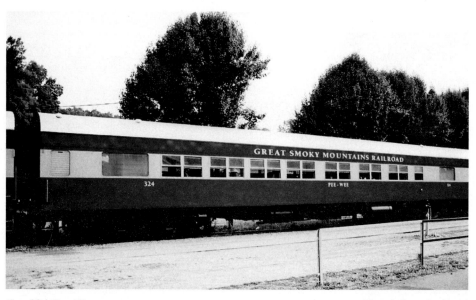

Car 324 Pee Wee.   *(Frank Strack photo)*

Car 324 Pee Wee

This car was built in 1921 and is also a heavyweight coach with three axle trucks. The original owner is believed to be the Nashville, Chattanooga and St. Louis and the car may have been used on the *City of Memphis*. Great Smoky Mountains Railway rebuilt it in 1989.

Car 522 Jackson

Number 522 is a heavyweight coach originally used in commuter ser-

Car 522 Jackson.   (Frank Strack photo)

Car 523 Cherokee.   (Michael George photo)

Car 536 MacNeill Club Car (formerly Powhattan Arrow).   *(Frank Strack photo)*

Car 822 Royal Palm.
(Frank Strack photo)

vice on Canadian National Railway. It has three axle trucks and was built in the thirties. Great Smoky Mountains Railway rebuilt the car in 1992.

Car 523 Cherokee
    Number 523 is a heavyweight coach originally used in commuter service on Canadian National Railway. It has three axle trucks and was built in the thirties. Great Smoky Mountains Railway rebuilt the car in 1992.

Car 3331 Champion
    Number 3331 was built in 1956 as a lightweight club car with two axle

Car 1103 Crescent Limited.   *(Frank Strack photo)*

trucks and used on Seaboard Air Line's *Silver Meteor*. It was restored to its original condition in 1994 by Great Smoky Mountains Railway.

Car 4201 Panama (no photo)

The Illinois Central had this dining car built in 1952. Great Smoky Mountains Railway restored it to original condition in 1994. It is a lightweight car with two axle trucks complete with operating kitchen.

Car 3331 Champion.   *(Michael George photo)*

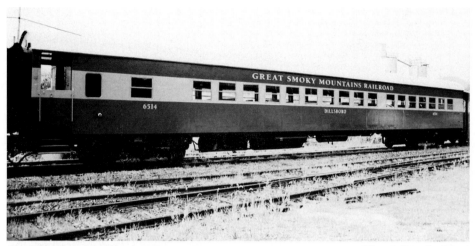

Car 6514 Dillsboro.   *(Frank Strack photo)*

Car 6514 Dillsboro

6514 is a lightweight coach that operated on the Chicago and North-western. It was built in 1952.

Car 8015 Silver Meteor.   *(Frank Strack photo)*

Car 8015 Silver Meteor

Number 8015 is a diner built in 1956 for the Seaboard Airline Railway. It was restored to its original condition in 1994 by Great Smoky Mountains Railway. It is a lightweight car with two axle trucks.

Car 8806 Dixie Flyer.   *(Michael George photo)*

Car 8806 Dixie Flyer
Built in 1949, this car operated on Atlantic Coast Line Railway as a diner. It has been restored to original Art-Deco style.

Car 8807 Conductor's Cafe
Built in 1949, this car also operated on the Atlantic Coast Line Railway as a dormitory. It is a lightweight car with two axle trucks. It was converted by Great Smoky Mountains Railway to a Cafe/Gift Store in 1998. It was owned by Amtrak for a while.

Car 8807 Conductor's Cafe.   *(Frank Strack photo)*

Car 536 MacNeill Club (before restoration)   *(Frank Strack photo)*

"Federail" baggage car painted and used in the movie, "My Fellow Americans" starring James Garner and Jack Lemmon.   *(Michael George photo)*

Open Cars

Five open cars, Whittier, Almond, Sarge Revis, Topton, and Olivine were once Kansas City Southern 70' baggage cars, all built in 1959. They were converted by Great Smoky Mountains Railway in 1993.

31 Almond Open Car   *(Frank Strack photo)*

34 Olivine Open Car   *(Frank Strack photo)*

Tuckasegee Open Car   *(Frank Strack photo)*

The Oconaluftee and Tuckasegee were once Norfolk and Western 56' flat cars built in 1964. They were converted by Great Smoky Mountains Railway in 1988.

Cabooses

Great Smoky Mountains Railroad owns several cabooses. Two cabooses have been converted to generator cars to provide electricity for the passenger cars. One came from the Atlanta and West Point but was originally L&N No. 6118. Another one, Generator car No. 1, was originally Wabash No. 2448. The Rio Grande, and GSMRR cabooses can be reserved for private parties. Several other cabooses have been converted to gift shops at the depots.

Generator Car No. 1. (Michael George photo)

Generator Car No. 2. (Frank Strack photo)

Chessie System Caboose No. 3753 has been converted to a rolling concession car and gift shop. (Frank Strack photo)

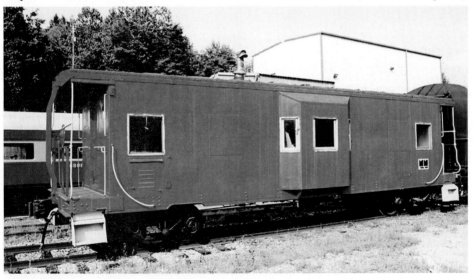

Asheville Chapter National Railway Historical Society caboose. Great Smoky Mountains Railroad sponsors NRHS functions over its railroad. (Frank Strack photo)

Rio Grande Caboose No. 01450 can be reserved for private parties. (Frank Strack photo)

Sante Fe Caboose No. 999447. Private caboose of Great Smoky Mountains Railroad owners, Allen and Carol Harper.   *(Frank Strack photo)*

The short tank car stores bunker oil for the steam locomotive. The larger tank car stores Diesel fuel. The cars are at Bryson City.   *(Michael George photo)*

Track maintenance equipment.   *(Michael George photo)*

John Stamper: Conductor

John began his railroad career on the Live Oak, Perry and Gulf Railroad while still in high school. He enlisted in the U.S. Navy in 1951 and served on several Air Craft Carriers as a radar operator with Anti-Submarine Squadron 21. After he was discharged, he returned to Live Oak, Perry and Gulf Railroad until going to work for the Seaboard Airline Railroad as trainman in 1956. He was promoted to conductor in 1960 and later to passenger conductor.

Conductor John Stamper getting ready to give the All Aboard.   *(Robert Royem photo)*

During 35 years of service with Seaboard he served on a local committee for the United Transportation Union and seven and a half years on the Board of Directors for the Seaboard Credit Union. John was also selected to work as trainman on the Presidential Campaign train known as the "Lady Bird Special."

John accepted early retirement from the CSX Railroad in 1991 with more than 42 years of railroad service and started work with the Great Smoky Mountains Railway in 1992 where he still works as conductor on the Tuckasegee River Excursion out of Dillsboro, N.C.

Chapter 6
The Natural View From the Train

Great Smoky Mountains Railroad runs through an area brushing the Great Smoky Mountains National Park to the north and the Nantahala National Forest to the south. This Southern Appalachian region is made up of summits and ravines richly diverse in climate and habitat, making for a wonderful mix of wildlife and vegetation. The

Rhododendron   *(Lavidge and Associates)*

abundance of water increases the beauty and helps insure the stability of life here. The following is presented as an overview of regional natural history.

Cultivated Fields and Borders

Few things in our mind's eye are as American looking as the cultivated fields of the farmer. Whether a field of tomatoes, broad leafed tobacco, soybeans or a stand of tasseled corn, the order and uniformity is charming. Along side the fields are the pasture lands with horses and cattle, possibly goats, donkeys and chickens. Do not ignore the rich opportunity to see wildlife and wild flowers in these areas. Pastures and the margin around tillage is teeming with interest.

Birds of the Fields

Northern Bobwhite (*Colinus virginianus*) a ground dweller, is at home in the tall weeds. These brown birds with white markings on the head are more readily heard than seen. Sometimes seen walking, either alone or in a covey, these small birds make quite a spectacle flying away in all directions if approached.

Killdeer (*Charadrius vociferus*) is another common bird who nests on the ground. Nest is a generous term for the killdeer. A nest may be in the center of a gravel driveway, just a depression in the rocks, but more likely it is in a grassy field. The male takes his turn during the incubation process, keeping the eggs warm and turned. Even with his help, the female stays close by to act out her deception of a broken wing if she senses her nest is in peril.

Red-winged Blackbird (*Agelaius phoeniceus*) a beautifully marked, easily identified bird with the male having the bright red shoulder patch. The female has streaks of light brown to assist her in camouflaging her nest in the bushes.

Red Tailed Hawk   (Carl Swafford)

Red-tailed Hawk (*Bueto jamaicensis*) perches high on a limb. Overlooking the farmer's field, the hawk will wait for a mouse or rabbit to have for breakfast. They can also be seen soaring overhead, their sharp turns showing the red of their tail. A good fight in flight between hawks and crows is always interesting. Though not as common, you may also see the **Broad-winged Hawk** (*Bueto platypterus*) and the smaller **Sharp-shinned Hawk** (*Accipiter striatus*).

Broad-winged Hawk
(Carl Swafford)

American Goldfinch (*Carduelis tristis*) is one you cannot miss. The small yellow bird is a bright spot on any fence post. They are also seen in flocks. They show up anywhere along the line, but in summer and early fall, look for them on the Bull Thistle at Mile Post 96.

Mourning Dove (*Zenaida macroura*) is a gentle bird who struts when walking and sounds like it needs to be oiled when taking off in flight. These soft gray birds with white edging visible on the tail feathers when in flight, are numerous in many places along the track. A similar bird, the **Rock Dove** (*Columba livia*) is also common here.

Turkey Vulture (*Cathartes aura*) is the largest soaring bird you will see. In flight they are magnificent. When encountered on the ground their size is startling. They, along with the smaller **Black Vulture** (*Coragyps atratus*) feed on carrion. They may be seen perched in large groups in dead trees or on power lines in the mornings. Keep a lookout for them around the Mile Post 98 area.

Many other birds inhabit the grassland and the edge of fields. They include **Eastern Bluebird** (*Sialia Sialis*), **Eastern Kingbird** (*Tyrannus tyrannus*), **Field Sparrow** (*Spizella pusilla*), **Mockingbird** (*Mimus polyglottos*) and the North Carolina state bird, **Northern Cardinal** (*Cardinalis cardinalis*).

Mammals of the Fields

Red Fox (*Vulpes vulpes*) is a shy secretive animal which you are more likely to see early mornings. They are just as happy to eat corn out of the farmer's field or a chicken out of his poultry yard. This is a beautiful canid whose color varies greatly from black to gray to the expected red. If you are lucky enough to spot one, look for the white-tipped tail, which is the marking of a red fox.

Woodchuck (*Marmota monax*) also called a groundhog or whistle pig is a very common sight. You may see one peeping out from under the Kudzu, or standing on a rock or stump in the sunshine. These animals burrow into the ground to make their homes and raise their young. It will make a special

Woodchuck   *(Carl Swafford)*

room in the burrow which it lines with grass and hibernate there for the winter. These cute little fur balls can ruin a garden but like most wildlife, it is worth the loss in corn and melons to see one.

White-tailed Deer (*Odocoileus virginianus*) a beautiful, peaceful sight, feeding at the edge of the field. These deer are numerous in the area and at times a hazard on the roadways. The young have no scent and may be left safely alone by the mother while she feeds some distance away. Should you come upon

White Tailed Deer
(Dale Taylor)

a lone fawn, do not disturb, Mom will come back for it shortly.

Eastern Spotted Skunk *(Spilogale putorius)* (If you neglect to read the scientific names on some of these you are missing a treat.) and **Striped Skunk** *(Mephitis mephitis)* both live in the region. The beauty of a skunk family bouncing along a trail or through a field, from the safety of the train of course, cannot be rightly conveyed. Their luxurious fur in contrasting colors shouts to be admired. Just admire from a distance. You will not need to be told twice.

Eastern Cottontail *(Sylvilagus floridanus)* is the common rabbit seen nibbling the green beans at the edge of the garden. The shorter eared **New England Cottontail** *(Sylvilagus transitionalis)* makes this region its home also, but their secretive ways keep them out of sight.

Coyote *(Canis latrans)* sightings during the daytime are not uncommon. The population has been increasing in the east for several years. Coyotes can be identified by the dark vertical line on their lower front legs and black tip of their tails.

Mixed Forests

The forested mountainous region that is home to Great Smoky Mountains Railroad is one of the most scenic in the United States. With a turn of the track you can go from warm sunlight with Oaks and Poplars to dark cool shade with Hemlocks and Rhododendron. The view out your train window also changes with the seasons.

Flowering Dogwood
(Lavidge and Associates)

Springtime brings a green mist to the region with the first budding leaves of the **Flowering Dogwood** *(Cornus florida)*. These are followed by their distinctive white flowers. Paired with the showy pink blooms of the **Eastern Redbud** *(Cercos canadensis)* these trees alone are enough to bring you back each Spring. Add to that the orange red buds of the **Red Maple** *(Acer rubrum)* and Spring is in the air.

With warmer weather comes the return of the Warblers. Two warblers worth looking for are the **Black-throated Blue Warbler** *(Dendroica*

Caerulescens) whose name says it all, and the **Blackburnian Warbler** *(Dendroica Fusca)* with striking black and white stripes and bright orange throat and cheek. The tiny **Ruby-throated Hummingbird** *(Archilochus colubris)* is the jewel of the air as it whizzes from flower to flower searching for the nectar that fuels its body. The mature male has the conspicuous red throat, the female is a metallic green.

Scarlet Tanager (Carl Swafford)

Springtime is also the time for the emerging of the **Black Bear** *(Ursus americanus)*. Mother bear will be particularly hungry now, nursing cubs having depleted her store of winter fat. They may eat the inside bark of trees, insects, small mammals, fish, or garbage from the dumpster. Bears have been sighted along the tracks. You might keep an eye out for them at Mile Post 89. While bears are a treat to see, and the young cubs are almost irresistible, please keep your distance.

Black Bear　　　　　*(Carl Swafford)*

In years past the bears were unrivaled in these woods. That changed in the early 1900's when **Wild Boars** *(Sus scrofa)* escaped into the wild here in North Carolina. They compete ferociously with the bears for food, having a detrimental effect on the bear population. They also do extensive damage to woodland vegetation.

Spring flowers along the track and in the forest are too numerous to list. From the lawn pest **Dandelion** to the elegant **Trillium**, there is never a lack of floral beauty. Several members of the Violet family can be found, including the eye-catching **Birdfoot Violet**, so named because of its foliage. The bright red of the **Fire Pinks** and **Indian Pinks** can not be missed. The cool blue/pink of the **Virginia Bluebells** and the

Dwarf Crested Iris.
(Michael George photo)

169

Lady Slipper   (Carl Swafford)

Fire Pinks (Michael George)

purple **Dwarf Crested Iris**, the **Wild Geranium** and the **Lady's Slipper's** pink add color and a softness to the woods. The scent of the **Honeysuckle** will be perfuming the air and **Oxeye Daisies** will be blooming everywhere. Soon the **Spring Beauty** and **Bloodroot** are gone and Summer is near.

The transition from Spring to Summer is signaled by the blooming of the **Mountain Laurel** (*Kalmia latifolia*), **Rosebay Rhododendron** (*Rhododendron maximum*), and **Catawba Rhododendron** (*Rhododendron catawbiense*). These lovely heaths bloom from Mile Post 49 at the Cowee Tunnel through the Nantahala Gorge and grow in thick stands on to Andrews.

Bloodroot   (Carl Swafford)

Summer in the mixed forests yields a sea of green. The Oaks have finally filled in their leaves. A wide variety of Oaks make identification fun. A general rule is rounded leaves and light colored bark indicate one of the White Oaks. These could be **Post Oak** (*Quercus stellata*) , **Chestnut Oak** (*Quercus prinus*), or **White Oak** (*Quercus alba*). These Oaks produce a crop of acorns every year. Pointed leaves and darker bark will likely be one of the Black Oaks which include **Pin Oak** (*Quercus palustrius*), **Scarlet Oak** (*Quercus coccinea*), or **Blackjack Oak** (*Quercus marilandica*). Black Oaks take two years for acorns to mature. Acorn production is very important as food for the wildlife of the Southern Appalachians.

Sourwood (*Oxydendrum arboreum*) graces the landscape in the heat of the Summer with beautiful Lily-of-the-valley like flowers. These flowering

Mountain Laurel
(Lavidge and Associates)

Rhododendron
(Lavidge and Associates)

trees are a treat for bees, being the source of that wonderful Sourwood honey. At the same time the **Silk Tree** (*Albizia julibrissin*), more commonly referred to as Mimosa, opens into fragrant pink blooms which continue through the Summer.

One Hundred years ago the **American Chestnut** (*Castanea dentata*) thrived here and produced a crop of chestnuts every year. An introduced fungus *Cryptonectria parasitica* has since killed the trees. Some places you can still see young shoots growing where the roots safely hide in the ground. Yet before reaching maturity, these too will succumb to the blight. Perhaps before these roots completely die scientists will find help for the American Chestnut and once again their thorny husks will litter the forest floor.

Dutchmans Britches
(Carl Swafford)

Pignut Hickory (*Carya glabra*) is one of the most common Hickories of the area. The **Red Hickory** (*Carya odorata*) and **Mockernut Hickory** (*Carya tomentosa*) also are here and with the Oaks and **Yellow Poplar** (*Liriodendron tulipifera*) make up a large portion of the canopy in the deciduous forest.

Black Locust (*Robinia pseudoacacia*) is widespread. Along the Tuckaseege River coming out of Dillsboro near Mile Post 48, you can see them growing with the **Sycamore** (*Platanus occidentalis*). There is an interesting contrast between the bark of the spiny Locust and the white peeling bark of the Sycamore. Also growing here are **Black Walnut** (*Juglans nigra*), and **Royal Paulownia** (*Paulownia tomentosa*). Both of these trees have fruit somewhat similar to the Sycamore. The major difference being that the Walnut is

171

quite tasty, the Sycamore is inedible, and the Paulownia is poisonous.

There are trees too numerous to mention, Elms, Birches, Mulberry, Ash, Tupelo, Sassafras, and many others. Grab a field guide and enjoy the ride.

Wild Turkeys (*Meleagris gallopavo*) are commonly sighted along the tracks. They may be spotted in numbers rummaging through the forest floor. Not as widely identified, the male **Ruffed Grouse** (*Bonasa umbellus*) stands and beats his wings, sounding like a lawnmower that never quite gets started. The warm brown **Wood Thrush** (*Hylocichla mustelina*) is here too, performing the

melodious songs of the woodland.

An amazing array of wildflowers blooms along the track. The track clearance allows just enough sunlight to spill in to enable most

Asiatic Dayflower of the Spiderwort family.
(Frank Strack photo)

Spiderwort
(Michael George)

of the flowers of the region to thrive within viewing distance of the train. **Spiderwort** blooms a lovely blue in the morning. Orange **Butterfly Weed, Queen Anne's Lace, Mullein, Jewel Weed, Cardinal Flower, Sow Thistle,** and **Morning Glory** commonly grace the edges of the woods. The beautiful **Purple flowering Raspberry, Wild Bergamot, Rose Vervain,** and **Passion Flower** vie for attention

Jewel Weed   *(Carl Swafford)*

Purple flowering Raspberry
(Carl Swafford)

Cardinal Flower.
(Michael George photo)

alongside the **Poke Weed** and **Spurge.**

Kudzu, prominent in several places, notably Mile Post 67, has redeeming qualities. It is here for erosion control. In late Summer the blooms are very fragrant. The flowers can be dried and used in pot pourri as they keep their deep purple color. Jelly can also be made from the blossoms.

Summer is a rich time for the deciduous forest, but could it be that the most wonderful time is just around the corner?

There is a crispness in the air as Fall mellows from one end of the track to the other. Then pristine Dogwoods which have been just another leaf in the understory burst into brilliance as do the Maples, Sassafras, Oaks and Tupelo. The leaves of the **Umbrella Magnolia** (*Magnolia tripetala*), large and dry, look like sheets of paper thrown throughout the forest floor.

Joe-Pye Weed, Asters, Black-eyed Susans, and **Goldenrod** finish the season with a flourish.

Black-eyed Susans. (Michael George photo)

Tall Ironweed is in the foreground and Rough-stemmed Goldenrod is in the background. (Michael George photo)

173

The **Gray Squirrel** (*Sciurus carolinensis*) and **Eastern Chipmunk** (*Tamias striatus*) are busily gathering Hickory nuts and acorns. One last rush of preparation before the cold of Winter sets in.

Winter is the best time to view the evergreens. **American Holly** (*Illex opaca*) is a wintertime favorite. With sharp, shiny green leaves and bright red berries, it is a treat for the eyes as well as a source of food for birds and other wildlife. **Eastern Red Cedar** (*Juniperus virginiana*) scaly leafed and tattered looking reddish bark, also a wildlife food source with its blueberry like fruit, is one of the most aromatic of the evergreen trees. Both **Eastern Hemlock** (*Tsuga canadensis*) and **Carolina Hemlock** (*Tsuga caroliniana*) can be found. Although they can be trimmed to form a hedge, when seen in their natural state, they are tall graceful trees reaching 60 feet. The miniature cones, no longer than 1.5 inches hanging from the ends of twigs add to their elegance. You will see them all along the track, but some lovely ones are at Mile Post 92 behind the barn.

Gray squirrel
(Carl Swafford)

While Pine trees are thought of as common, the **Table Mountain Pine** *Pinus pungens*) is found only in the Appalachians. It has small cones with thick downward curved spines that stay on the tree several years past maturity. Other pine trees include the **Eastern White Pine** (*Pinus strobuss*), easily identifiable by its icy blue green needles and elongated cone, **Pitch Pine** (*Pinus rigida*) and **Shortleaf Pine** (*Pinus echinata*). To give it its proper respect, it should be noted that the Pine is the North Carolina state tree.

A light dusting of snow or glaze of ice makes any of these trees a delightful Winter scene. Now there will be deer and rabbit tracks in the snow and chickadees will nibble Hemlock seeds. Now is the time for the forest floor to be nourished by the bright sunlight, feeding and drawing Spring flowers from their sleep. Soon, the cycle will begin again.

Raccoon   *(Carl Swafford)*

Waterways

Pleasant accompaniment for any of the rides is the bountiful waterways. Whether Valley River or Fontana Lake, the rushing Nantahala or the Tuckasegee, the sight is refreshing. Fish are abundant and the fishing is good, especially for the birds. The **Great Blue Heron** (*Ardea herodias*) is an unmistakable local fisherman although the smaller **Green Heron** (*Butorides striatus*) is more common. You may also see the **Belted Kingfisher** (*Megaceryle alcyon*) hover and then quickly dive into the water to take his meal. If you completely

Great Blue Heron
(Carl Swafford)

miss out on the birds, there will be ducks behind the train station in Dillsboro.

Screech Owl
(Carl Swafford)

Night Life

Night time has a special beauty all its own. The fragrance of the **Honeysuckle,** or **Mimosa**, or **Kudzu** is more keen. The **Whip-poor-will** (*Caprimulgus vociferus*) can be heard along with the scream of the **Bobcat** (*Felis rufus*). **Lightning Bugs** (fireflies) dance up from the ground and soar among the trees, their beauty reflected in the river. The **Screech Owl** (*Otus asio*) and **Barred Owl** (*Strix varia*) can be identified by their calls. **Raccoons** (*Procyon lotor*) prowl for food in the dim light, and the **Luna Moth** silently locates a place to deposit her eggs. The **Jack-o-lantern mushrooms** (*Clitocybe illudens*) delight children of all ages with a pale green glow. Come find the beauty unique to its own season and time here with us at Great Smoky Mountains Railroad.

Bibliography

Books

Harrison, Fairfax, *A History of the Legal Development of the Railroad System of Southern Railway Company,* Washington, DC, 1901.

Hyde, John B., *Second Supplement to Legal History of the Lines of Railroad of Southern Railway Company,* Washington, DC, 1958.

Newton, Louis M., *Rails Remembered Volume 1,* Roanoke, VA, Progress Press, Inc., 1992.

Periodicals

Calvert, W. N., Jr., "Relocation of the Southern Railway Above the Fontana Reservoir," *Engineering News Record,* December 16, 1943, pp. 78-82.

Clodfelter, Frank, "Saluda," *Trains,* November 1984, p. 26.

Monroe, Herbert G., "Murphy Branch," *Railroad Magazine,* June 1949, pp.32-59.

Monroe, Herbert G., "Rails Across the Blue Ridge," *Railroad Magazine,* December 1943, pp.8-29.

Monroe, Herbert G., "Skyline Dispatcher," *Railroad Magazine,* May 1946, pp. 8-31.

Reed, G.Warren, "The Southern Railway's Murphy Branch," *Model Railroader*, Vol. 51, no. 10, October 1984, pp. 32-59.

Ties, November 1951, pp. 9-13

Wrinn, Jim, "The Murphy Branch . . . A Report on its Demise and Resurrection and a Look Back at the Murphy Line," *The Green Light,* July-August 1988, pp. 1-5.

Other Publications

Contract Between Tennessee Valley Authority and Southern Railway Co., June 17, 1943.

Great Smoky Mountains Railway Souvenir and Coupon Book

ICC Locomotive Accident Reports

Southern News Bulletin-September, 1923, p. 3.

Supplemental Agreement Between TVA and Southern Railway Co., Dec. 11, 1952.

Docket AB-290, Southern Railway Abandonment, March 31, 1988.

Notes

[1] Herbert G. Monroe, "Murphy Branch," *Railroad Magazine,* p. 32.
[2] Ibid., p.33.
[3] Fairfax Harrison, *A History of the Legal Development of the Railroad System of Southern Railway Co.,* p. 293
[4] Ibid., p. 294.
[5] Herbert Monroe, "Murphy Branch," p. 37.
[6] Ibid.
[7] Ibid., p. 39.
[8] ibid.
[9] Ibid., p. 42.
[10] Ibid.
[11] Fairfax Harrison, *A History of the Legal Development of the Railroad System of Southern Railway Co.,* p. 301.
[12] Frank Clodfelter, "Saluda," p. 26.
[12a] Herbert G. Monroe, "Murphy Branch," pp. 43, 44.
[13] Ibid., p. 44.
[14] Ibid., p. 45.
[15] Jim Wrinn, "The Murphy Branch... A Report on its Demise and Resurrection and a Look Back at the Murphy Line," *The Green Light*, p. 3.
[16] Herbert G. Monroe, "Murphy Branch," p. 45.
[17] Ibid., p. 46.
[18] Ibid., pp. 46, 47.
[19] Ibid.
[20] Ibid., pp. 48, 49.
[21] Ibid., p. 50.
[23] Ibid.
[24] Ibid., pp. 51, 52.
[27] G. Warren Reed, *Model Railroader,* October 1984.
[28] Herbert G. Monroe, "Skyline Dispatcher," *Railroad Magazine,* May, 1946.
[29] Great Smoky Mountain Railway Souvenir Book p. 29.
[30] Herbert Monroe, "Murphy Branch," p. 57.
[31] Jim Wrinn, "The Murphy Branch... A Report on its Demise and Resurrection and a Look Back at the Murphy Line," *The Green Light*, pp. 1, 5.
[32] Ibid.
[33] TVA, *The Fontana Project.,* p. 44.
[34] Ibid., p. 505.
[35] Louis M. Newton, *Rails Remembered, Volume 1*, p. 170.
[36] Ibid.
[37] Ibid.
[38] W. N. Calvert, "Relocation of the Southern Railway Above the Fontana Reservoir," p. 78.
[39] Ibid., p. 79.
[40] Contract between Tennessee Valley Authourity and Southern Railway, pp. 3-5.
[41] Ibid., pp. 5, 6.
[42] TVA, *The Fontana Project*, pp. 503, 504.
[43] Ibid., p. 502.
[44] Ibid., p. 507.
[45] Ibid., p. 505.
[46] W. N. Calvert, "Relocation of the Southern Railway Above the Fontana Reservoir," p. 80.
[47] Ibid., p. 81.
[48] Ibid., p. 79.
[49] Ibid., p. 79, 80.
[50] TVA, *The Fontana Project*, pp. 247, 248
[51] John B. Hyde, *Second Supplement to Legal History of the Lines of Railroad of Southern Railway Company,* pp. 172, 273, 274, and 552.